THE BATTLE FOR THE FAMILY

BY Tim LaHaye

The Battle for the Family

Tim LaHaye

FLEMING H. REVELL COMPANY
OLD TAPPAN, NEW JERSEY

Unless otherwise identified, Scripture quotations are from the King James Version of the Bible.

Scripture quotations identified NAS are from the New American Standard Bible, © The Lockman Foundation 1960, 1962, 1963, 1968, 1971, 1973, 1975.

Scripture quotations identified NKJV-NT are from the New King James Bible–New Testament. Copyright © 1979, Thomas Nelson, Inc., Publishers.

Those who wish to use the original artwork in teaching the principles in this book are invited to write for a transparency catalog: Family Life Seminars, Post Office Box 1299, El Cajon, CA 92022

Quotations for THE HUMANIST MANIFESTO © Prometheus Books, Inc., 700 E. Amherst St., Buffalo, N.Y. 14215.

Ron Aldridge's article, in chapter five, is reprinted by permission of the Chicago Tribune-New York News Syndicate, Inc.

ISBN 0-8007-1277-3

To Margaret Palmer LaHaye, who when widowed at age twenty-eight, refused to give up her seven-week-old son, her five-year-old daughter, and the author, who was almost ten. Totally unskilled at the time, rejected by welfare, helped by her relatives, she worked, slaved, prayed, sacrificed, and loved us into adulthood.

For Peggy White, of Denver, Colorado; Dick LaHaye and myself, of El Cajon, California; and your thirteen grandchildren and eight great-grandchildren scattered everywhere, we say: "We love you! and want to pass on to our children's children the great heritage you gave to us."

May God bless you in this life and the one to come is our prayer.

Acknowledgments

This book would not have been possible without the dedicated efforts of my secretary, Connie Horn, who typed my handwritten notes; Dr. James DeSaegher, my dear friend and an English professor who edits all my writings; and Marvin Ross, the artist who so graphically captured my thoughts in portraying the symbols throughout.

Contents

THE BATTLE FOR THE FAMILY

1

The Importance of the Family

Will your family and the families of those you love survive the closing decades of the twentieth century? Probably not, unless you take definite steps to preserve them. Today the family is breaking down at a faster rate than at any time in human history.

Divorce, the ultimate step in family destruction, has reached epi-

demic proportions, and no one is immune. The number of family breakups doubled between 1970 and 1980. Although this decline in the family slowed somewhat during 1980, if the rate of the past ten years continues, permanent marriages will soon drop to below 50 percent of the population.

One phenomenon of the 70s has been the increase in divorce of those married for more than twenty years. Just a few years ago the notion prevailed that if a couple made it through two decades, their marriage was sealed for life. But that is no longer true. Now it is alarmingly common to hear of families falling apart after the last child leaves home.

Civilization is changing at a dizzying pace, and couples often mature quite differently. Consequently the happy lovers of eighteen, who had so much in common, are often strangers at thirty-eight. This is particularly true in homes where one is an avid reader and the other is not; they just grow apart. It is also true when one partner becomes a committed Christian and the other does not.

A century ago that wasn't very important for two reasons: There wasn't all that much to read, and the average life span was only thirty-four for men and thirty-nine for women. Today it is sixty-three for men and sixty-nine for women. In just one hundred years the prospects of a couple living long enough to celebrate their fiftieth wedding anniversary have increased several times—if they don't become a divorce statistic. Years ago a poor marriage could be endured for twenty years, but today couples are taking a different look at a bleak prospect that could last fifty years.

Christians Are Not Exempt

Just a few years ago divorce was rare among Christians. In the Michigan congregation of my boyhood, I can remember only one divorced couple. Today the epidemic is assaulting even the church. A startling number of veteran Christians are choosing divorce as a solution to marital difficulties, instead of facing them as a sign of spiritual problems that with God's help, could be resolved. An increased number of divorced people are found in the church today because so many exciting conversions are taking place, and many individuals turn to the church after a family breakup. Others are drawn to the church for counseling to solve family disharmony, and all too often only one partner will receive Christ. This circumstance will not automatically provoke a divorce, for the new babe in Christ may strengthen the relationship; yet at times the unbeliever will reject both the partner and his newfound faith.

If the truth were known, of all the institutions, the church has done the most to preserve the family. The church not only instructs and enriches the lives of those who attend its services, but provides many excellent sources of biblical counseling. Our own church counseling center, with God's help, has salvaged over five hundred couples who have come to us for help. That effect can be multiplied by hundreds of like-minded churches.

That isn't the whole story. In all honesty I must acknowledge that even among Christians raised and married in the church, divorce is accelerating at an alarming rate. As the battle against the home rages outside, some of the attacks that destroy the marriages of the nonchurched are devastating an ever-increasing number of church homes.

Unfortunately, many churches no longer practice church discipline or invoke biblical standards for the permanence of the home. Divorce is becoming so commonplace that some churches even permit Christians who sought unbiblical divorces to hold high church offices, contrary to the Scriptures; they even accept a minister who divorced his wife for another woman. Recently I was saddened, while attending a Christian booksellers' convention, to find three Christian celebrities sporting new wives. Strangely enough, it does not seem to hurt their ministries, even though they do not reflect a spirit of repentance. Evidently some Christians have two standards of conduct: one for the celebrity and one for the average person. That is blatantly unscriptural; God's dealing with King David ought to teach us that.

These comments should not be construed as suggesting that God does not forgive our sins and our blunders, but without repentance, He can never absolve our transgressions! From the very beginning God intended marriage to be for life. One of the best preventives against divorce is to accept that fact. As we shall see, as far back as

anthropology will take us, marriage has always been entered as a
lifetime contract. Divorce and separation were the exception, not
the rule. Today's family breakdown is a phenomenon largely limited to the past century.

The History of the Family

The family has always existed. As far back as we can trace re-
corded history, we find this institution. It is as old as the book of
Job, written about 400 years before Abraham. If you know the
story, you remember that it concerns a husband, wife, and fourteen
children. They had a home, friends, animals, work, trials, sickness,
joys, and heartaches. Not much has changed in the five thousand
years since Mr. & Mrs. Job lived.

Even before that, Adam and Eve, the special creations of God,
were brought together in marriage by God Himself. He not only
commanded them to "... Be fruitful, and multiply, and replenish
the earth ..." (Genesis 1:28), but instructed them, even before in-
laws existed, that each couple inhabit its own home. "For this cause
a man shall leave his father and his mother, and shall cleave to his
wife; and they shall become one flesh" (Genesis 2:24 NAS).

The Bible, then, establishes the essential pattern for the prehis-
toric existence of marriage, and its testimony is corroborated by the
story of anthropology.

> In every branch of written history, whether that of ancient Egypt,
> ancient China, medieval Europe, or modern America, the record
> shows that the family has been the vehicle through which men and
> women have entered upon life. In the family they have been born,
> there they have been trained to take a place in society as adults, and
> from there they go out to begin the cycle all over again with their
> own children. Even more significant as a measure of the antiquity
> and fundamental nature of the family is that anthropological stud-
> ies of cultures far removed in character from so-called civilized so-
> cieties have turned up virtually none which lacked a family life.[1]

This does not preclude significant changes of life-style within the
family. For example, affectional marriage—that is, couples who are
drawn to marriage by a mutual love—are of more recent vintage.

For most of the world's history, parents selected the spouses of their young, who developed love relationships after marriage. That may not sound exciting to modern citizens of the Western world, but even where that practice is in effect today (India, Africa, the Orient, and some places in South America), homes are more stable than in our own culture.

The family has faced additional historical, cultural, and economic changes. For example, prior to the Industrial Revolution it was common for wives to work out in the fields, along with the men; this system was a matter of survival, as in parts of India and China today. Not until the Industrial Revolution did men earn enough pay to fully support their families, enabling the wives to stay at home and be the homemakers and chief teachers of their young.

The number of children in a family has also changed through the years. In past ages the family held as many children as the woman's body could produce (in some cases as many as twenty-five); according to the recent census, the United States now averages 1.6 children per family.

For most of the world's history, juvenile crime was nonexistent. Young people were so busy working in the fields, to eke out a bare existence, that they did not have the free time that so often spawns trouble.

Yes, the family has experienced many changes due to race, culture, religion, and other factors, but there has never been a time when the family was not a functional unit within society. Anthropologist George P. Murdock, who analyzed some five hundred cultures, found only one society that lacked the basic family unit as we know it, and it is extinct! That rare exception is worth a closer inspection.

The Nayars of southern India, in fact, no longer exist as a living culture, so what anthropologists know about them comes from what can be remembered by the people in the area, none of whom live as the Nayars did. Among the Nayars paternity was apparently a one-night thing, offspring being reared by the mother and her female relatives. The actual father of the child was usually not known, since the mother willingly accepted passing visitors as sexual partners. Since the "visiting husbands" came only at night, the relationships hardly involved either a marriage or a common residence. The relationship also lacked any permanence or rights of parentage since all that was expected of the "visiting husband" who acknowledged paternity was that he pay the costs of the midwife! Beyond that there were no reciprocal economic obligations between the parents.[2]

No wonder they became extinct! God's plan for the family is the only one that works.

What Is a Family?

Believe it or not, the most costly department of the federal government (Health, Education and Welfare), when commissioning the 1980 President's Council on the White House Conference on Families, could not even agree on a definition for the family. This, of course, was due to their mental commitment to secular humanism.

In his book *At Odds: Women and the Family in America,* Dr. Carl Degler, developing a historical framework, lists five essential elements for the family, based on the best anthropological research. "Very few societies" have ever lacked these basics:

1. The family "begins with a ritual between a woman and a man, a ceremony that we call marriage, and which implies long duration, if not permanence, for the relationship."[3]
2. The marriage partners "have duties and rights of parenthood that are also socially recognized and defined. For the family has everywhere been the way in which the human being is socialized. There are several other ways to prepare children for adulthood, to be sure, but all of them are very recent in origin (orphanage, kibbutz, commune), and around none of them has a whole society yet been organized."[4]
3. The components of a marriage—husband, wife, and children—"live in a common place." This has been true 75 percent of the time; in the other cultures, the husband lived away from the family for part of the time—as in the case of

polygamy—but in most of these he did not live very far away.[5]

4. "... there are reciprocal economic obligations between husband and wife—that is, they both work for the family, even though the amount and kind of labor or production may be far from equal."[6]

   It should be pointed out that until recent times, the wife worked either in the home or in the fields or orchards adjacent to it. In most cases she was able to take her nursing or very young children with her.

5. "... the family also serves as a means of sexual satisfaction for the partners...."[7]

Do those characteristics sound familiar? They should, for they describe what we mean by the expression the *traditional family*. The profamily movement that speaks for at least 85 percent of the American people currently defines *family* as "a man and woman bound by marriage, living together with their children by blood or adoption." Even Alvin Toffler identifies the traditional family as "a husband-breadwinner, a wife-housekeeper, and a number of small children."[8] Essentially that represents the biblical definition of a family, often referred to as the Judeo-Christian concept because it dates from the beginning of mankind. I like the term *traditional family*.

Today that traditional-family definition, like the family itself, is in serious jeopardy! Many of the radical activist groups that seem to exercise an inordinate influence over government bureaucrats, the media, and particularly education are determined to include homosexuals, lesbians, and singles living together without benefit of marriage in their new definition of a *family*. For such "families," they demand full legal status and the same benefits as members of traditional families.

One tactic of these radicals displays their incredible bias: their distorted finding that only 7 percent of America's families consist of a working father, a mother-homemaker who does not work outside the home, and their two children. After that statistic was publicized, these groups used their finding to mean that only 7 percent of

America's families qualify as traditional families. This statement is all part of their carefully designed plan to transform the meaning of the traditional-family concept and to have their definition proclaimed as the version of family life in America.

To clarify how distorted the radicals' thinking has become, we need only consider how that narrow 7 percent interpretation of family excludes the following members of the traditional family:

Couples with only one child
Couples with three or more children
Couples with a mother working out of the home and with two children
Couples with a working mother and one, three, or more children
Couples whose children have graduated from the home
Couples who never had children
Couples with adult singles living at home
Widows and widowers
Divorced parents raising their children at home

90 percent of America

Admittedly all Americans do not now live in a home where only the father works and there are two children. My own family would not presently qualify on that basis, for Bev now works out of the home, and our four children have graduated to their own homes. But like the overwhelming majority of people in the Western world, we accept and still consider ourselves to be part of the traditional family: that is, a man and woman, committed to each other by marriage, with such children as may be related to them by blood or adoption.

Any doubt that we are a traditional family and that children are our greatest treasure would be erased if you could look in on our favorite vacation. For six consecutive years, Bev and I have rented a giant houseboat at Lake Powell and invited our children, their spouses, and our grandchildren to join us as we pull our ski boat, jet skis, and other water toys for our annual family vacation. For two weeks we push from our minds the writing of books, our church, Family Life Seminars, Concerned Women for America, and many other activities, in order to enjoy our family. Frankly, those two weeks give fulfillment and purpose to the frantic pace we maintain the other fifty weeks. Most people can identify with that, for family is the most important part of anyone's life.

Loneliness and the Antifamily Movement

During the past four years three publishers have urged me to write a book on loneliness. Were it not for what I consider more pressing subjects, I would have done so, for loneliness is certainly an urgent problem. One of the reasons that millions suffer such pain today is the increasing loss of family life.

As the number of singles delaying marriage or rejecting it altogether has risen, it is estimated that 20 percent of today's adults do not share their lives with another.[9] Divorce, abandonment, and death add to this trend, causing many others to live a solitary life. The increased suicide level of such singles clearly indicates that it is a more lonely life-style than that of people who enjoy the intimacy of a family. Admittedly people may be lonely even in a family, but the percentage of lonely people is several times higher for those outside the family unit.

I find it interesting that in the Bible, God arranged for all individuals to live within a family. Singles were to remain at home until marriage. (Isaac, for instance, was forty years old and still living at home before he married.) If a man died, his wife was to be taken into his brother's family or returned to her father's house, but no one was to go on alone. God has given everyone an intuitive craving for fellowship. The contemporary "me" generation neglects that instinct at its own peril.

Alvin Toffler, in his recent book *The Third Wave,* explains:

> ... we are witnessing a population explosion of "solos"—people who live alone, outside a family altogether. Between 1970 and 1978 the number of persons aged fourteen to thirty-four who lived alone nearly tripled in the United States—rising from 1.5 million to 4.3 million. Today, a fifth of all households in the United States con-

sists of a person living solo. Nor are all these people losers or loners, forced into the solo life. Many deliberately choose it, at least for a time.[10]

The Importance of the Family

There is no substitute for the family! It will never be replaced. Admittedly many of the elite humanists who have worked their way into key positions of influence in our government and educational system are doing everything they can to discredit and destroy family life today, but they will not succeed. However, our society is experiencing a sociological shift. Instead of living together without marriage, couples have started the fad of the 80s: child-free families. According to Toffler, at the turn of the century few couples remained childless, and singles living alone were rare. By 1970 "only one in three adults lived in a home with children under eighteen." In 1960 2 percent of the families went childless, but that percentage jumped 60 percent in just fifteen years.[11]

As dangerous as these trends seem, we shall discover that they are only well-orchestrated fads that because of the heartache, confusion and futility they cause, will eventually be discarded. Marriage and family are still the favorite life-style of the overwhelming majority. If the divorce rate is really 44 percent, that still means 56 percent of the married couples remain married to one person. But even that is only part of the story, for a *U.S. News & World Report* study of marriage and divorce indicates that 94 percent of those who divorce marry again! It is safe to say that 88 percent or more of our population will choose marriage over the single life.

The Purpose of the Family

Amid all the modern discussion of marriage, we seem to have lost sight of the real purpose for marriage and the family. It was not designed by our Creator only for companionship, sexual activity, or even for fulfillment. The primary purpose was to raise children, for without that the human race would soon become extinct. To put it in proper perspective, let's highlight three purposes for the family, suggested by Michael Novak, nationally respected reporter and syndicated columnist.

1. The primary purpose of the family is to raise children. God commanded the first married couple to "... Be fruitful, and multiply, and replenish the earth ..." (Genesis 1:28).

Mankind does not have the power to create. We can only manufacture out of that which God has created. The closest we can come to the God-like characteristics of creation is procreation of another human being like ourselves: a child with a free will, eternal soul, and the capacity to generate another life in due time. The mystery of procreation is that the child comes out of the womb part mother and part father. Ideally children should be a product of their parents' love; a natural identity with their parents should be a means of bonding for life, and these ties should be with cords of love.

Michael Novak described the importance of the family for child raising this way:

> Why the family? ... First, without it there isn't any future. It is as simple as that. There is only one way for the human race to have a future. That is for us to have children. If we should all stop having children the human race ends when the last of us dies.[12]

In some influential quarters, child raising is made to sound like drudgery to be avoided at all costs. Instead of recognizing that "children are an heritage of the Lord. ... Happy is the man that hath his quiver full of them ..." (Psalms 127:3, 5), the current fad postulates, "Have your own career, limit or delay a family as long as possible, and don't let children inhibit your freedom."

Bev and I had four children, and we would be the first to admit that they hampered our freedom, sapped our energy, and drained our bank account. But they were worth every bit of it! Children are a blessing, but a couple wrapped up in themselves and their activities will never enjoy "the little people." Today thousands of the brainwashed victims of our humanistically controlled society are trading the love of unborn children for "me-ism" and their own "personal rights."

2. The second purpose of the family is to provide each person in the home with opportunities for individual development. When

population experts talk about the 4 billion people on planet Earth, they tend to forget that these 4 billion individuals need identity, acceptance, encouragement, development, and love in order to fulfill their highest potentials in life. No government on earth can provide such care. But our Creator has designed one institution in which such necessities can be provided: the family.

One reason I know the family will never be replaced is that only in the family can a child or adult receive the necessary individual care that will help him accept himself, his sex, his skills, and his purpose for living. Dr. James Dobson, associate clinical professor of pediatrics at the University of Southern California School of Medicine, teaches that everyone gains his self-acceptance from outside himself.[13] The Christian family is the best place for such learning; here the individual starts to learn of God's acceptance, through faith in Christ; then he receives parental approval, then that of brothers and sisters, relatives, teachers, and others. An unwanted child, rejected by his parents, will encounter severe difficulty with self-acceptance, which is essential to emotional maturity; he will find it difficult to love and trust other human beings. There just is no substitute for loving parents! In fact, one parent can do the job. My father died when I was nine, my sister was five, and my brother was seven weeks old. We never knew what it was like not to be loved, and we acknowledge that our sense of self-acceptance today is largely due to sacrificial mother love. Today she is loved by thirteen grandchildren and six great-grandchildren—a resounding tribute to the concept of *family*.

3. The third purpose of the family is to teach moral values. What you are morally is what you are. Morals directly affect judgment, attitude, and values; they also influence motivation.

Take, for example, the subject of authority. If a person does not properly understand the relationship of obedience to authority and personal freedom, he is not equipped to face life. Humanistic educators' obsession with human rights, total freedom, self-expression, and self-actualization has bred a disrespect for authority that destroys freedom. You cannot have true freedom in society without respect for authority. Total freedom always leads to anarchy, which is followed by totalitarianism and the loss of freedom. This occurs individually as well as collectively. If you don't believe that, interview some of the inmates at Folsom Prison. Desiring total freedom, they have lost all freedom.

No adult is prepared to face the uncertainties and challenges of life until he understands that he will never be truly free until he has learned a respect for authority and a willingness to submit to it. The ideal place to learn that is in the family. Only two commands in the Bible are directed to children (*see* Ephesians 6:1, 2):

1. Obey your parents in the Lord.
2. Honor your father and your mother.

In my opinion, the best authority on child raising in the last three hundred years was Mrs. Susanna Wesley, the mother of seventeen living children, two of whom (John and Charles) shook both England and America for God. John Wesley could well be credited with saving America from a form of eighteenth-century hedonism and ushering in the Great Awakening. Mrs. Wesley is often quoted as saying, "The child that never learns to obey his parents in the home will not obey God or man out of the home."

Parents have not fulfilled their obligation to God, to their children, to society, and to themselves if they fail to teach their children that true freedom, enjoyed over a lifetime, must include a healthy respect for authority and the rights of others. That is a vital purpose of the family! But there is more. Children must learn moral rights and wrongs, which contrary to popular humanistic theories, are absolute. A child's natural IQ, skills, and potential will be seriously limited if he is not indoctrinated with the time-honored moral values of integrity, virtue, honesty, industry, and self-discipline. These values are best learned before he is five years of age; from then on they become increasingly hard to appropriate, particularly if the child is subjected to a public-school education, which insures a moral-valueless education.

Many parents who do not invest the time and energy necessary to develop the above qualities in their children try later to compensate for this lack of attention by spending $20,000 or more to buy a college education for them. Their efforts may simply produce another undisciplined, unprincipled, valueless college graduate. In many cases the education only serves to make the early childhood failure more dangerous.

The family was designed by the Creator to help us avoid these pitfalls. No wonder Dr. Harold Voth of the Menninger Foundation has said, "Our civilization is headed for collapse if we don't start caring more for our children and strengthening family life."

The Key to Family Survival

General George S. Patton, Commander of the United States Third Army, was the greatest field commander of World War II. His repeated victories over Field Marshal Erwin Rommel were a testimony to the fact that the first step toward victory over an enemy of any kind is to know him. You cannot fight what you do not know or understand. Patton had studied the German military mind until he could anticipate every major move.

Today the family is being assaulted from without by at least fifteen mortal enemies. Homes are being destroyed and children wasted because millions of parents do not even realize that their family's life is under attack. Viewing with disbelief the soaring crime rate; the alarming increase in teenage pregnancy; and the promiscuous sexual activity of our young, which is accepted as a normal life-style, mom and dad shudder and try to forget. But when the front-page headlines scream "College Suicides Raging," and when suicides are escalating on both the high-school and junior-high level, they find it extremely frightening. Equally alarming is the fact that VD among twenty-four-year-olds has become the nation's number-one health hazard and herpes simplex of the genitals is incurable. Unfortunately the attacks on the family today are so vicious and varied—from drugs to perversion—that many have turned from the battle and focused their attention upon other things. Not until the wall collapses and crushes their teen does the truth come home: The family today is in greater jeopardy than at any time in history.

THE FIFTEEN ENEMIES OF THE FAMILY

The Fifteen Forces of Evil

I have been a family counselor for thirty years, twenty of them with special emphasis on marriage counseling. Ten years ago I founded Family Life Seminars (FLS), a special teaching ministry, through churches, to strengthen family life. Together with some of the country's outstanding family speakers, like Dr. Henry Brandt, Dr. Howard Hendricks, and Dr. Ken Poure, for the last five years my wife, Beverly, and I have conducted over 375 seminars on family living, provided training for over 300 thousand people. FLS has branched out into cassettes; movies; counseling by mail; radio; temperament tests; book distribution; and a COM (cassette of the month), the largest family-life cassette club in the country, featuring many of the nation's leading authorities on family subjects.

I rehearse these developments, not to impress you, but to clarify that family is my business. I have spent a major portion of my life studying and helping families.

During these years I have paid careful attention to the causes for the increase in human family tragedies. As the war has heated up, particularly in the past five years, I have listed the distinct forces that are attacking the family. In my other books I have addressed the internal problems of the family, but in this one I want you to see the fifteen malevolent forces that are inexorably working toward the destruction of the modern family. Every home is vulnerable to any or all of them, depending on the age, number, and interests of each family member. Some are worse than others.

It is my purpose to acquaint you with each of these forces before calling your attention to the many resources that can insulate your family against such attack. Like a series of battles in a war, one attack does not comprise the entire war. You may even lose one or two battles and still win the war. But if you fail to recognize the existence of your attackers, you will not be prepared, and the enemy will destroy your most precious possession: your family. Good family life is more difficult today than ever in history; this dilemma will intensify as we draw ever closer to the twenty-first century, particularly if the humanistic forces that have launched most of these attacks are permitted to control the most influential agencies in our society.

One preliminary warning: Don't become discouraged as we march through the fifteen forces that relentlessly attack your family. Remember, He that is in you is greater than he that is in the world. There is still hope for your family, but it will only be realized when you fully understand the nature and extent of the enemy. I am confident that families that comprehend the reality of these enemies can take positive steps to insulate theirs against them.

Let's begin with the most powerful and subtle enemy of all.

Notes

1. Carl N. Degler, *At Odds: Women and the Family in America* (New York: Oxford University Press, 1980), p. 3.
2. *Ibid.,* p. 4.
3. *Ibid.,* p. 3.

4. *Ibid.,* p. 3.
5. *Ibid.,* pp. 3, 4.
6. *Ibid.,* p. 4.
7. *Ibid.,* p. 4.
8. Alvin Toffler, *The Third Wave* (New York: William Morrow and Company, 1980), p. 225.
9. *Ibid.,* p. 228.
10. *Ibid.,* p. 228.
11. *Ibid.,* p. 229.
12. Michael Novak, "The American Family: An Embattled Institution," *The Human Life Review* 6 (Winter 1980), p. 45.
13. James Dobson, *Hide or Seek,* rev. ed. (Old Tappan, N.J.: Fleming H. Revell Company, 1979), p. 60.

2

Humanism: Family Enemy Number One

With its many tentacles extending eagerly from such centers as government, public schools, TV, and pornographic-literature sources, the octopus of humanism is determined to destroy the fam-

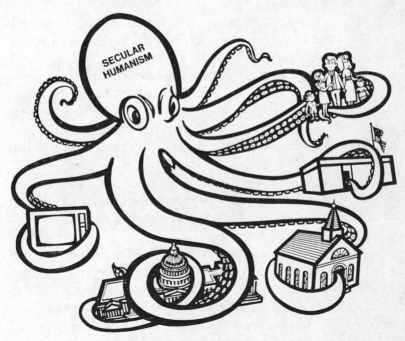

ily. Yet many Christians are not even aware of its existence. Secular humanism is an anti-Christian system of thought that influences every decision and most of a person's actions. It is anti-God, anti-moral, anti-self-restraint, and anti-American. Amazingly, humanism often masquerades as humanitarianism. In reality, there is nothing humanitarian about it, because its beliefs make it antihuman.

In our colleges and universities, secular humanism is regarded with respect that borders on awe, whereas in reality it is responsible for most of the ills of today's society. A seventeen-year-old boy was killed in our city by a motorist whose car went out of control because he was smoking marijuana. He didn't see the lad on the back of his friend's bicycle. Who is to blame? The humanist professors, whose salaries we pay, who brainwashed an entire generation of young people with the unscientific notion that "pot" was good and should be legalized!

Or consider the twenty-one-year-old woman who sat weeping in my office after a hysterectomy operation that cost her the opportunity of ever becoming a mother. Whom do you blame for the humanistic sex-education teacher who encouraged her class of fourteen-year-olds to become "sexually active" but never warned them that girls who are promiscuous before eighteen are *five times* more vulnerable to cancer of the cervix and 100 percent more vulnerable to VD, pregnancy, and herpes simplex virus type 2 than virgins?

From the conflict between parents and youth, created by its "new morality," to the strife between mates, inspired by its feminist movement, humanism has to be labeled family enemy number one. Fortunately in the last three years an amazing, spontaneous educational process in America has opened the eyes of millions of fundamental Christians, pro-lifers, and others whose religious and moral beliefs originate in the Bible. Unconditional war has been declared; antimoral humanism and historic Christianity are in a struggle for survival, with the traditional family at stake. If humanism prevails and achieves the goal, outlined in the *Humanist Manifesto II,* of turning this country into a humanistic nation by the year 2000, the family will die. If we Christians win (as I thoroughly believe we will, assuming we can educate enough of our citizens), family life will bounce back stronger than ever.

When I wrote *The Battle for the Mind,* it was almost like giving birth to a child. For years I had been aware of the evil that humanistic control was exercising over my beloved nation. That is why I founded two educational institutions, established a family ministry, and assisted Dr. Henry Morris in founding the Institute for Creation Research. Whenever I had opportunity to speak to ministers or Christian school teachers on the subject, I found them extremely responsive. But between 1976 and 1980 I watched a professing Christian become president of the United States and then surround himself with a host of humanistic cabinet members, assistants, judges, and almost three thousand other humanist appointees. These people nearly destroyed our nation and, given another four years, might have plunged us into another French Revolution, only this time on American soil. In the process it would have destroyed the American home.

We still aren't out of the woods, of course, which is why I am anxious to produce a series of books that expose humanism as the most fraudulently evil religion in our country today. I can appreciate how the great writer Aleksandr Solzhenitsyn must have felt after he came to America and spoke out in print to warn the West of Communism's systematic destruction of his homeland. Unlike Solzhenitsyn, I am attempting to delineate what you can do to safeguard your home from the evil effects of humanism and stop its uninhibited control of our society. After preaching six Sunday-night messages on the subject, in both locations of our church in San Diego, I discovered that my congregation was as deeply concerned for America as I was—so much so that they paid for the mailers and the postage as Bev and I, with help from our publishers and some of our other friends around the country, sent free copies of my first book on this subject to over 85,000 pastors throughout the nation, asking them to teach its concepts to their congregations. The measure of our church's enthusiasm was demonstrated by their response to our call for 500 volunteers to spend all day at one of our gymnasiums, to package and prepare the books for mailing. So many people responded that we ran out of space and had to send 135 home. The response to our church's message of concern, sent to the other Bible-believing churches in the land, has been exciting. Thousands of ministers have written for the transparencies to use with the book, and bookstores can't keep it in stock. The funniest response came from a woman in Minneapolis, who heard me speak on humanism at a religious broadcaster's convention and accused me of using her pastor's series of sermons. Gradually people are waking up!

What Is Humanism?

Dr. Bill Bright, national director of Campus Crusade for Christ, who knows the college and university scene as well as anyone in the country, says:

> ... I believe the most dangerous religion is humanism ... humanism has become the greatest threat to our Judeo-Christian heritage and is doing more to destroy the moral and spiritual fiber of our society than any other peril.
> Have you ever wondered why our society is becoming more secular, why prayer and Bible reading are no longer welcome at our public schools? The religion of humanism is largely responsible. Have you wondered why Americans are much more tolerant today of sexual freedom, homosexuality, incest and abortion? The religion of humanism is largely responsible.[1]

Dr. Francis Schaeffer, the West's leading Christian philosopher, contends, "In our time, humanism has replaced Christianity as the consensus of the West."[2]

Aleksandr Solzhenitsyn shocked the academic society in 1978, when addressing the graduating class at Harvard University (a leading humanist think tank), by issuing a broadside at humanist thought.

> ... Solzhenitsyn criticized western values and proclaimed that "destructive and irresponsible individual freedom has been granted boundless space." The primary problem in Solzhenitsyn's opinion was the rise of humanism. "Such a tilt of freedom in the direction of evil has come about gradually, but it was evidently born primarily out of a humanistic and benevolent concept according to which

there is no evil inherent to human nature; the world belongs to mankind and all the defects of life are caused by wrong social systems which must be corrected. . . ."[3]

Dr. Paul Kurtz, editor of *Humanist Manifesto II,* noted, in 1975, when humanists thought it was safe to "let it all hang out":

Humanist attitudes are becoming more firmly established in our society. When first enunciated in the 1930s, humanism was considered a radical thesis in religion. It has since been widely accepted by millions of people, even within the churches. . . . Many of the old taboos have been undermined; freer, more open attitudes toward sexuality, sex education, abortion, euthanasia, marriage, divorce and birth control have developed.[4]

One sign of man's fallen nature is his universal tendency to be arrogant and egotistical. That very tendency, of course, may yet prove to be the humanist's undoing. Positive that they had gained an irreversible stranglehold on our nation's schools, government, media, and other major agencies that influence the thinking of America, they became vocal enough to awaken many of us from our lethargy. However their egotism caused them to underestimate the power of the church and traditional moral values, so as they freely teach their value-free beliefs, they now resent it when we point out their responsibility for the amoral practices of current society.

On November 4, 1980, no one was more amazed than the humanist leaders that ten flaming liberals of the United States Senate, consistently voting the anti-moral humanist line, were overwhelmingly ejected. Suddenly, on talk shows and in periodicals, these men started to disassociate themselves from humanism as it really is. As long as they could deceive people into considering their decisions and activities humanitarian, the battle was easy. Now that millions of people are waking up to the fact that they are not humanitarian in the least, they face a rough road ahead. Personally I can't wait to see what they will do when millions more in our culture begin to realize that humanism is today's greatest threat to the family. When that happens, our citizens will throw off the controlling tentacles of humanism, until traditional moral values can be legally reinstated and moral sanity and physical safety can once again return to our land.

Simply stated, humanism is a man-centered religion that mistakenly thinks it can solve the problems of man, independent of God. In reality humanism causes and compounds these problems. For a complete description of humanism's tenets, please read the first volume in this series, *Battle for the Mind*. In preparation for that book I read the works of many humanistic authors and reduced their teaching to the following basic beliefs that are authenticated by *Humanist Manifesto I* (1933) and *Humanist Manifesto II* (1973), documents signed by many university presidents, scholars, professors, writers, ministers, and other persons of influence. It is difficult for them to disregard these as official *beliefs* of humanism. Whether or not they like to admit it, *Humanist Manifesto I* and *II* are to humanists what the Bible is to us.

Consider the following quotes:

ON RELIGION

We believe, however, that traditional dogmatic or authoritarian religions that place revelation, God, ritual, or creed above human needs and experience do a disservice to the human species.

We find insufficient evidence for belief in the existence of a supernatural; it is either meaningless or irrelevant to the question of the survival and fulfillment of the human race. As non-theists we begin with humans, not God, nature, not deity.

No deity will save us; we must save ourselves.

Promises of immortal salvation or fear of external damnation are both illusory and harmful. They distract humans from present concerns, from self-actualization, and from rectifying social injustices.

There is no credible evidence that life survives the death of the body.

Traditional religions are surely not the only obstacles to human progress.

ETHICS

We affirm that moral values derive their source from human experience. Ethics is autonomous and situational, needing no theological or ideological sanction. Ethics stems from human need and interest.

ON THE INDIVIDUAL

We believe in maximum individual autonomy consonant with social responsibility. Although science can account for the causes of behavior, the possibilities of individual freedom of choice exist in human life and should be increased.

We believe that intolerant attitudes, often cultivated by orthodox religions and puritanical cultures, unduly repress sexual conduct. The right to birth control, abortion, and divorce should be recognized.

ON DEMOCRATIC SOCIETY

All persons should have a voice in developing the values and goals that determine their lives.

People are more important than decalogues, rules, proscriptions, or regulations.

The state should encourage maximum freedom for different moral, political, religious, and social values in society.

The principle of moral equality must be furthered through elimination of all discrimination based upon race, religion, sex, age or national origin.

Practicing humanists should make it their vocation to humanize personal relations.

We are critical of sexism or sexual chauvinism—male or female. We believe in equal rights for both women and men to fulfill their unique careers and potentialities as they see fit, free of invidious discrimination.

ON WORLD COMMUNITY

We deplore the division of humankind on nationalistic grounds. We have reached a turning point in human history where the best option is to transcend the limits of national sovereignty and to move toward the building of a world community in which all sectors of the human family can participate. Thus we look to the development of a system of world law and a world order based upon transnational federal government.

For the first time in human history, no part of humankind can be isolated from any other. Each person's future is in some way linked to all. We thus reaffirm a commitment to the building of world community, at the same time recognizing that this commits us to some hard choices.

We believe in the peaceful adjudication of differences by international courts and by the development of the arts of negotiation and compromise. War is obsolete. So is the use of nuclear, biological and chemical weapons. It is a planetary imperative to reduce the level of military expenditures and turn these savings to peaceful and people-oriented uses.

The same document from which the above quotes were taken calls humanism a religion. Nine times they flatly admit that their beliefs are a religion. Yet their religion is the official philosophy of today's public schools.

These five basic beliefs of humanism have increasingly influenced our society. They represent the approved religious doctrines of public education from kindergarten through grade school. They likewise account for the moral filth prevalent on TV and the unsafe condition of city streets. They help to explain why America has been reduced to a second-rate power, and they are the single, most destructive force of evil working to destroy the family today.

That does not mean that all humanists are committed to evil. Many whom I have met were indeed very nice people: family oriented, faithful partners and conscientious parents. However that is not a result of humanism, but a carryover from the traditional moral values that they adopted from our Judeo-Christian culture. Whether or not he is personally committed to evil, the humanist's decisions, conclusions, and plans will advance humanism, not the good of America.

The biblical principle "As a man thinks in his heart, so is he," is just as appropriate for a humanist as it is for a Christian. A humanistic philosophy of life will color a person's entire thinking process. This was illustrated in a debate I had with former Senator Frank Church on "The David Susskind Show." He could not get over the fact that he was pictured by conservatives as an evil person because of his voting record. He could not, or would not, comprehend that the conservative-minded people of his state were not unmindful of his good family life or his reportedly clean personal moral life. They objected to him because his voting record favored the liberal humanist line, not the traditional moral values embraced by the majority of the people of his state. He was voted out of office because of his voting record, not his personal life, as every public official who holds a humanist view of man, God, government, and the world should be.

To better perceive how totally humanism determines a person's decisions, carefully examine the following diagram:

HUMANIST PRE-SUPPOSITIONS

MENTAL CONCLUSIONS

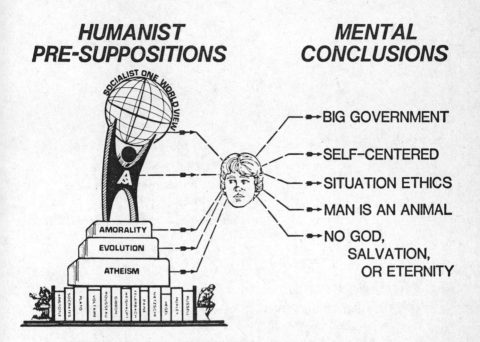

The conclusions, decisions, and objectives of humanists are almost always contrary to those who hold traditional moral values, primarily because humanism's presuppositions or beliefs are 180° in opposition to the Judeo-Christian ethic. That is why so much antifamily conflict abounds in our country today. To appreciate that fully, examine the traditionalist or conservative presuppositions.

The beliefs of those who hold traditional moral values are well-known to fundamental Christians, for they have been their chief exponent in America. However, they are shared by many others: Jews, Catholics, Mormons, and members of most Western religions. By contrast, Eastern religions are prone to be more humanistic. In fact they form the source for most theories or beliefs of humanism.

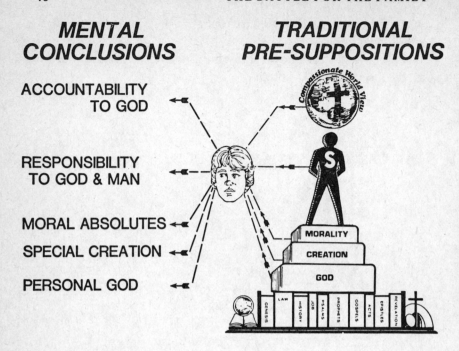

MENTAL CONCLUSIONS

ACCOUNTABILITY TO GOD

RESPONSIBILITY TO GOD & MAN

MORAL ABSOLUTES

SPECIAL CREATION

PERSONAL GOD

TRADITIONAL PRE-SUPPOSITIONS

Compassionate World View

MORALITY

CREATION

GOD

GENESIS · LAW · HISTORY · JOB · PSALMS · PROPHETS · GOSPELS · ACTS · EPISTLES · REVELATION

Traditional theological tenets include:

1. The belief in God.
2. Creation by the direct act of God. (Some have been duped by evolutionary teachers and have conceived what they call *theistic evolution* or a God-guided evolution. Such individuals, who, in the face of so little scientific evidence for evolution, have adopted this position, should study the case for *scientific creationism.*[5])
3. Man is morally responsible to obey God's written law.
4. Man's chief aim: to serve God.
5. A compassionate world view that prepares man for eternity.

Surprisingly enough, there is little difference among traditionalists when it comes to these five basic beliefs, which serve as the foundation for our American culture. Admittedly those numerous theological or religious beliefs wherein we disagree have produced over 400 different denominations, religious groups, cults, and associations in this land of religious liberty. But traditional moralists almost universally agree that these five concepts are necessary to maintain a morally sane society.

Shades of Humanism

Not all humanists are alike. As I began debating them, I quickly discovered that humanism is a philosophical religious movement that has as many differences or degrees as one finds among Christians. To label a person Christian is to utilize broad religious terminology. One may mean Baptist, Presbyterian, Lutheran, or some other denomination or group. And within each denomination we can usually find a broad spectrum from evangelical to liberal. So it is with humanism. I would label some humanists *committed humanists,* that is, they believe all five of the points I have described, commit their lives to them, and usually seek to impose them on our culture. Right of them would be *liberals* or *liberal humanists,* and if we go far enough to the right, we come to the *humanized Christian.* The chart on the next page should put this in perspective.

The battle for the future of America will be fought between committed humanists on the one hand and committed Christians on the other. Those in between will often get in the way of both sides. They are important, however, for they comprise the objects of the warfare and hold the millions of votes that will decide who will be our governors, leaders, and lawmakers of the future.

Ironically, the smallest army (the humanists) has the mightiest weapons, humanly speaking: government leadership and money, education, and media. This is why they appear to be in the majority. The biggest army (the church and her many agencies, along with millions of other moralists and special-interest groups) is fighting with its back against the wall, as if the survival of our culture is at stake; and it is. But these troops are not alone. God visited them with an unexpected breath of freedom on November 4, 1980, because they prayed and worked hard at waking up their fellow citizens. If we keep working, He will again do for our country what He did for England and America in the eighteenth century, under the preaching of John and Charles Wesley. If we can awaken enough

COMMITTED HUMANIST	LIBERAL HUMANISTS	HUMANIST VICTIM
Indoctrinaire, hardcore five-pointer who aggressively pursues humanistic goals Probably signed *Humanist Manifesto I* or *II*, belongs to American Humanist Association, writes, teaches, or in some way is "involved" in the movement May or may not be Marxist but is not uncomfortable with that philosophical persuasion Can be counted on to vote and work for liberal causes and vigorously oppose moral absolutes	Family-oriented, patriotic person who has been exposed to humanism throughout his schooling, has thought very little about religion or moral values Basically wants his family to be raised in a moral environment but does not realize that humanist policies will destroy his family Usually votes for liberals and does not understand why the country is getting so evil	Believes and often lives like a committed humanist but is not overly aggressive about it Very idealistic, if a teacher or writer, will include humanistic teachings in his work Probably not comfortable with Marxists but does not realize they think alike Opposes traditional morals as too restrictive, usually votes for liberals
CHRISTIANIZED HUMANIST	**HUMANIZED CHRISTIAN**	**COMMITTED CHRISTIAN**
Family-oriented, patriotic, industrious person who, though he may not be religious, is respectful of those who are and shares many of their moral values but does not realize that these values came from Christianity or Judaism. A law-abiding citizen who tends to vote conservative more than liberal depending on the candidate and his understanding of the issues	Family-oriented patriotic person who has been exposed to humanism throughout his schooling, has thought very little about religion or moral values Basically wants his family to be raised in a moral environment but does not realize that humanist policies will destroy his family Usually votes for liberals and does not understand why the country is getting so evil	A dedicated Christian with strong moral values, a patriotic person who is usually concerned about the moral breakdown around him Opposes abortion, pornography and other practices that violate Biblical values that are important to him, depending on how often he studies the Word of God Usually votes for those who share his moral values

citizens who will humble themselves before God, so that we, as a people, will repent of our national sins and prayerfully seek His ways, He will again hear from heaven and heal our land by sending us Great Awakening II. The future belongs to those who will prayerfully work for it. I have to believe that Christians are more motivated than humanists, now that we are waking up to the fact that a war is raging about us and that our families and our country are at stake.

I find it encouraging that so many groups throughout the country are calling millions of our countrymen to prayer and repentance by educating them on the dangers of religious humanism. One group, Concerned Women for America, has set a goal of 50,000 prayer chapters, with chains of from 300 to 350 women in every city and district in the country. Nothing is more powerful than prayer.

In my first book on humanism, *The Battle for the Mind,* I pointed out that humanism's value system is not shared by the majority of the American people, according to George Gallup's most thorough survey of religious life in America. According to that report, 84 percent believe that the Ten Commandments are still valid for today. This means that a minority of humanists are leading the majority of citizens. But how can that be? Very simple. During the past ten years they have infiltrated the most important institutions in our culture, until they literally exercise more influence on our laws, education, news media, entertainment, and many other activities than do the majority who are pro-moral, profamily and pro-life.

The charts on the next three pages illustrate this inordinate influence.

Proof of Humanism s Bankruptcy

America was founded upon a biblical base of thought, which produced the highest level of living, best educational system, and greatest degree of freedom in any country in the history of the world. For the past forty years, this base, usually referred to as *traditional moral values,* has been replaced in government, education, and the media by the amoral values of secular humanism. Official government policy during this time shows clear signs of humanistic thinking, and education has been almost totally controlled by hu-

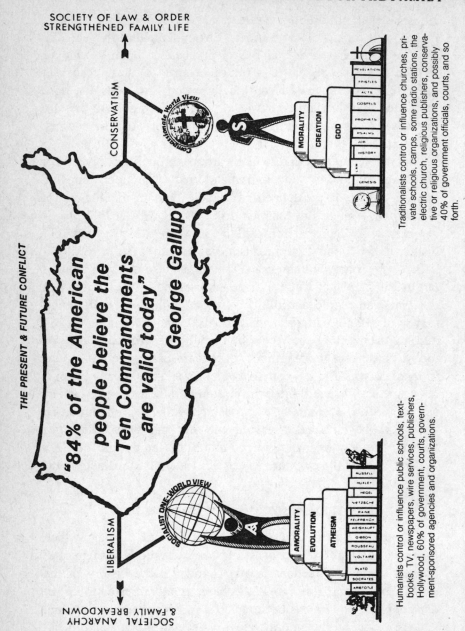

SOCIETY OF LAW & ORDER
STRENGTHENED FAMILY LIFE

CONSERVATISM

THE PRESENT & FUTURE CONFLICT

"84% of the American
people believe the
Ten Commandments
are valid today"
George Gallup

LIBERALISM

SOCIETAL ANARCHY
& FAMILY BREAKDOWN

Traditionalists control or influence churches, private schools, camps, some radio stations, the electric church, religious publishers, conservative or religious organizations, and possibly 40% of government officials, courts, and so forth.

Humanists control or influence public schools, textbooks, TV, newspapers, wire services, publishers, Hollywood, 60% of government, courts, government-sponsored agencies and organizations.

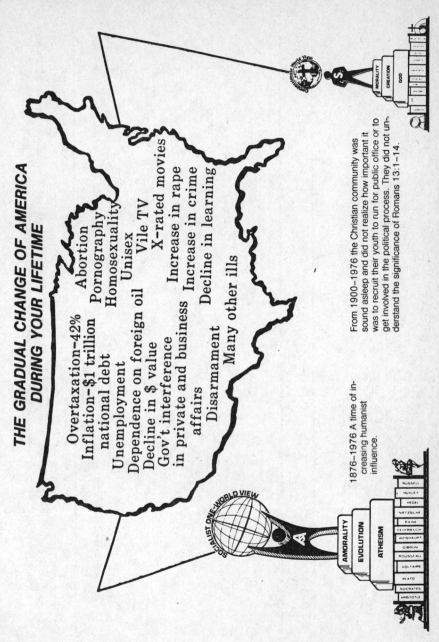

THE GRADUAL CHANGE OF AMERICA DURING YOUR LIFETIME

Overtaxation–42%   Abortion
Inflation–$1 trillion   Pornography
national debt   Homosexuality
Unemployment   Unisex
Dependence on foreign oil   Vile TV
Decline in $ value   X-rated movies
Gov't interference   Increase in rape
in private and business   Increase in crime
affairs   Decline in learning
Disarmament   Many other ills

MORALITY
CREATION
GOD

From 1900–1976 the Christian community was sound asleep and did not realize how important it was to recruit their youth to run for public office or to get involved in the political process. They did not understand the significance of Romans 13:1–14.

1876–1976 A time of increasing humanist influence.

SOCIALIST ONE-WORLD VIEW

AMORALITY
EVOLUTION
ATHEISM

RUSSELL
HUXLEY
HEGEL
NIETZSCHE
PAINE
FEUERBACH
WEISHAUPT
GIBBON
ROUSSEAU
VOLTAIRE
PLATO
SOCRATES
ARISTOTLE

The chart on the next page shows the time line of presidents and some of the laws humanists have introduced that have changed the face of America.

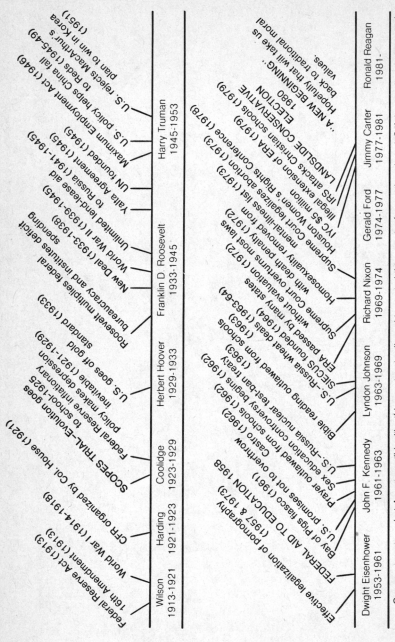

Wilson
1913-1921

Federal Reserve Act (1913)
16th Amendment (1913)
World War I (1914-1918)
CFR organized by Col. House (1921)

Harding
1921-1923

SCOPES TRIAL–Evolution goes to school-1925
Federal Reserve inflationary policy makes depression inevitable (1921-1929)

Coolidge
1923-1929

U.S. goes off gold standard (1933)
Roosevelt multiplies federal bureaucracy and institutes federal deficit spending
New Deal (1933-1938)

Herbert Hoover
1929-1933

World War II (1939-1945)
Unlimited lend-lease to Russia (1941-1945)
Yalta Agreement (1945)
UN founded (1945)
Maximum Employment Act (1946)

Franklin D. Roosevelt
1933-1945

U.S. policy helps China fall to Reds (1945-49)
U.S. rejects MacArthur's plan to win in Korea (1951)

Harry Truman
1945-1953

Dwight Eisenhower
1953-1961

FEDERAL AID TO EDUCATION 1958
Bay of pigs fiasco (1961)
U.S. promises not to overthrow Castro (1961)
Sex education outlawed from schools (1962)
Prayer outlawed from schools (1963)
Bible reading outlawed from schools (1963)
U.S.–Russia nuclear test-ban treaty (1962)

John F. Kennedy
1961-1963

SIECUS founded (1964)
U.S.-Russia wheat deals (1963-64)
ERA passed by many states without Supreme Court evaluation (1972)

Lyndon Johnson
1963-1969

Homosexuality removed from mental-illness list (1972)
Supreme Court legalizes abortion (1973)
Supreme Court overturns most laws with death penalty (1972)

Richard Nixon
1969-1974

Houston Women's Rights Conference (1978)
IYC $5 million extension of ERA (1979)
IRS attacks Christian schools (1979)
Illegal legalizes abortion (1973)

Gerald Ford
1974-1977

Jimmy Carter
1977-1981

LANDSLIDE CONSERVATIVE ELECTION 1980
"A NEW BEGINNING."
Hopefully that will take us back to traditional moral values.

Ronald Reagan
1981-

Can you imagine what America will be like if humanism is allowed to control this country for another decade? If they realize their goal of making this a humanist country by the year 2000, we will either have revolution or a dictatorship. As Dr. Francis Schaeffer teaches, humanism leads to a moral breakdown, destroys the family, and ushers in civil chaos followed by dictatorship. Consider the French Revolution: Humanism brought in pornography, prostitution, a breakdown in the family, crime increased and led to revolution by Napoleon Bonaparte.

Effective legalization of pornography (1957 & 1973)

manists and the media. Both TV and the press are dominated by those favoring liberal humanism and antagonistic toward those who espouse traditional moral values.

The best way to assess the bankruptcy of humanism's theories is to point out that during the same period of time (1941–1981), even though the government has quadrupled in size, it is less able to protect its citizens from violence and crime; it has turned the world's superpower into a second-rate nation that fears its inability to withstand an attack by the Soviet Union.

The cost of education has skyrocketed, so that today's education costs more than eight times as much as it would have in 1941, but learning effectiveness has decreased significantly. TV programming has become so immoral that it is being turned off by the majority of the population.

If humanism was really good for mankind, we would expect 1981 living conditions to be better than those in 1941. Granted, we do have faster cars; better means of communication and technology; and multimillion-dollar schools, colleges, and universities, but the quality of life has deteriorated drastically. When streets are no longer safe, crime is out of control, and inflation threatens the economic existence of many families, the quality of life has deteriorated. When elderly people who have faithfully paid into a social-security system for the forty years of their working careers have no confidence that it will provide for them in their old age (as promised by the liberal humanist theorists back in 1941), the quality of life has indeed deteriorated.

Humanists blame this tragedy on inflation, overpopulation, insufficient money for more government programs, and so on, but the real reason is that humanism is a failure. Its theories, which sounded so promising at first, do not work. They have never improved living conditions anywhere in the world, and life in America in the 80s is a daily testimony that the theories of humanism are *bankrupt.*

Presuppositions Affect Your Decisions

Without apology I acknowledge that all my conclusions are influenced by my Christian presuppositions or values. So are a humanist's, whether or not he will admit it. Usually he tries to claim that Christians are not objective, because of our religious presuppositions, whereas humanists are objective or "scientific." That is ridiculous! Everyone is influenced by his presuppositions. A humanist thinks like a humanist; a Christian thinks like a Christian. They will almost always be in conflict.

For example, a humanist maintains a *low* view of human life. Since he presumes that man evolved and is an animal, he can live like one. If a woman has an unwanted pregnancy, she may freely abort it, for an embryo is only a living mass.

By contrast, a Christian demands a *high* view of human life. That is, he was created by God in His own image, with an eternal soul, a free will, and the capacity to pass faith on to future generations. For that reason, an unwanted fetus must not be aborted, for it is a creation of God.

The thinking processes of a humanist and a Christian will always be 180° in opposition on moral issues. Humanists, for example, be-

lieve that children should be free to be sexually active, whereas Christians totally reject that. This difference, which encompasses every subject we discuss with humanists, should not surprise us, for the Bible teaches, "Man's ways are not God's ways, and God's ways are not man's ways" (*see* Isaiah 55:8). The same premise appears in the New Testament, where the Apostle Paul first clarifies the difference between man's wisdom (humanism as he knew it in first-century Greece) and

God's wisdom as seen in the Scriptures (study 1 Corinthians 1:18–31). "But the natural man does not receive the things of the Spirit of God, for they are foolishness to him; nor can he know them, because they are spiritually discerned" (1 Corinthians 2:14 NKJV–NT).

Whenever I debate a humanist or liberal politician, I know in advance that we will contravene each other on every subject. That is why I oppose liberal humanism. It is contrary to the Word of God and will destroy our country if permitted to control our laws.

America is a free country, as you know; therefore humanists should be permitted to live and work here. But America must resolve that humanists are unfit to make our laws, serve as our government leaders, teach our young, determine the moral standards of our literature and TV entertainment, or interpret our news. Unfortunately for our nation, they do; and strangely enough, we pay their salaries.

Fortunately, a rapidly increasing number of our countrymen are waking up to the fact that we are at war with humanist thought and that although humanists presently control the government, the educational system, and our means of communication, they are a minority that is hopelessly out of step with the overwhelming majority of our people. They exposed their excessive misuse of power when they legalized abortion, resulting in the mass murder of 10 million unborn babies; turned San Francisco into a venereal-diseased jungle, like Sodom and Gomorrah; flooded our land with $5 billion worth of pornography, annually; and encouraged unmarried teens to sexual activity. Such policies, viewed by those committed to traditional moral values, borders on intellectual insanity. Yet we pay the salaries of such people to teach our young, make our laws, and judge over us.

How, you may ask, did all this come about? Very gradually over the past one hundred years. And it will take many more years to rid our nation of this secular-humanist influence, but it is happening as we educate enough people about the true nature of humanism. When enough people perceive what humanism really stands for, recognizing it as the source of most of our nation's ills and our families' mortal enemy, they will expel it from our schools, government, newsstands, and communications systems.

Personally I am encouraged. *The Battle for the Mind,* which is only one vehicle for exposing humanism, has enjoyed the best distribution in the shortest period of time of any of my books, because when people read it, they immediately buy copies for their friends. A Houston home builder gave out 5,000 copies, as did a Dallas businesswoman. Many ministers have ordered quantities for their congregations; others have purchased the transparencies to help teach their church families. During the first nine months of publication, 290,000 books have been shipped to bookstores. That is almost twice as strong a volume sale as any of my other fifteen books, all of which were considered best-sellers. Clearly, people are concerned and know that if we can awaken enough of our people, we will yet see America returned to moral sanity.

The Humanists Fight Back

Humanism has been exposed in magazine articles, on radio and TV, in movies, and in countless newsletters that are mailed out by the millions. I detect signs that the leaders of the humanist movement are running scared. They probably realize that their programs became blatantly excessive, and they have failed to reckon with the band of ministers, Christian laymen, and other traditional moralists who will stand up to them and oppose their harmful teachings and policies.

In Buffalo, New York, they have founded a new organization called the Council for Democratic and Secular Humanism, established in 1980. I have a copy of their first quarterly, called *Free Inquiry,* edited by Paul Kurtz, chief humanist spokesman and editor of *Humanist* magazine, which is the official house organ of the American Humanist Association. In it he states:

> This first issue of *Free Inquiry* is devoted primarily to a defense of democratic secular humanism.
> The Fundamentalist Right is gaining ground in the United States—which is symptomatic of the worldwide growth of funda-

mentalist and doctrinaire thinking—and its scapegoat is secular humanism.

The fundamentalists have attacked the basis of the democratic state, the principle of separation of church and state, and humanist views on ethics, religion, science, evolution, and education.

Since there has not yet been an adequate response, we are devoting virtually this entire issue of *Free Inquiry* to answer these attacks.[6]

Learn a lesson in the humanistic use of semantics, an art they mastered long ago. They regularly use a familiar word that means one thing to the population at large and another to a humanist. *Democratic secular humanism* sounds so noble and positive. Let me show you what it means.

Democratic = Unlimited freedom A totally amoral, free-literature society, and so on. What they do not say is that, historically, amorality always leads to chaos and anarchy.

Secular = Godless or atheistic

Humanism = *Manism* or "man is the center of all things," which leads to the worship of man, the ultimate in selfishness.

Properly translated, then, *democratic secular humanism,* the new banner under which humanists intend to parade their ideology to make it appear more respectable, really means "free, amoral, atheistic manism." I don't blame them for calling it democratic secular humanism; it sounds so much better than what it really is. But I assure you, their semantics will fool no one; we moralists will see to that.

Humanism Is Antifamily

Almost every teaching of humanism is contrary to the good of the family—from permissiveness, which emanated from humanistic psychology; to value-free, explicit sex education; the advocacy of child's rights over parents' rights; and the many other forces of evil working toward the destruction of the family. Don't be discouraged, however! There are solutions and safeguards that you can take to insulate your family against these evils; these will be covered in future chapters. But you need to be aware of the agencies humanism has turned against your family and nation, in order to oppose them. There are fourteen other tentacles to this monstrous humanist octopus, some of which you may not even recognize as a threat to your family.

Notes

1. Bill Bright, "Humanism . . . the Grand Delusion," *Worldwide Challenge* 8 (March 1981), p. 6.
2. Cindy Baum, Dave Boehi, and Jim Lowe, "Look What They're Doing to Our Minds," *Worldwide Challenge* 8 (March 1981), p. 12.
3. *Ibid.,* pp. 10, 12.
4. *Ibid.,* p. 12.
5. For information, write the Institution for Creation Research, 2100 Greenfield Drive, El Cajon, CA 92021.
6. Paul Kurtz, "About This Issue," *Free Inquiry* 1 (Winter 1980/81), p. 2.

Government: Friend or Foe?

America has enjoyed the longest period of free elections of any nation in world history. For this reason most of our citizens had

confidence in their government, until we entered the 70s. But with increasing disillusionment, that confidence has waned until, on a roster of professions scaled from one to twenty-four, the people who were polled listed politicians as number twenty-three, one notch above used-car salesmen.

A 1980 survey entitled "Is Government Helping or Hurting American Families?" received 46,817 responses, 92 percent of which indicated that government was harmful to the family. Those surveyed stated that official government policies "weaken rather than strengthen family bonds.... Our middle-class families are angry and frustrated about government. They feel their pockets are being picked, their opinions ignored, their wants overlooked and unfulfilled."[1] Those feelings are certainly justified, and they probably comprise the principal reason for the rejection of the liberal (big-government) administration of Jimmy Carter in 1980.

Overtaxation

Government is expensive! Because government is out of control, it costs the family dearly, simply because an elite group of bureaucrats, politicians, and superliberal humanist judges are changing our laws, regulations, and policies to suit their desires and theories, not to suit the wants or needs of the American people. And the federal government is not the only culprit: State, local, city, and county governments also have their hands in our pockets. It is estimated that 42 percent of the average working man's salary is spent on taxes.

A *U.S. News & World Report* article stated that the average American works until May tenth each year just to pay his taxes; but that isn't the whole story, for we pay taxes on taxes. The same article pointed out that we pay 109 taxes on a loaf of bread. For instance, the farmer has to charge extra to pay his personal taxes and the taxes he pays on fertilizer, seed, gasoline, equipment, trucking, utilities, and services; the baker is forced to pass along his property, withholding, and inventory taxes, as do the distributor and supermarket.

Instead of treating these taxes with respect, because of the personal sacrifice on the part of most taxpayers, government bureaucrats display a callous attitude as they waste our money. The first time I heard that government employees purchase vast quantities of supplies and services at the end of each fiscal year so that their chances for an increase in appropriations the next year would not be jeopardized, I was horrified. Now that turns out to be only the tip of the iceberg.

Former Secretary of Health, Education and Welfare Joseph Califano admitted to a Senate investigative committee that he could not even account for 6 to 9 *billion dollars* of our tax money. Somehow the fact that he was in charge of the third largest budget in the world (third only to the whole budget of the United States government and that of the Soviet Union) didn't reassure me. Since the average American will pay $7,000 in federal taxes alone this year, it would seem that bureaucrats could find some way of becoming better stewards of our money.

In *Fat City: How Washington Wastes Your Taxes,* author Donald Lambro, a reporter for United Press International, accuses government bureaucrats of squandering "$100 billion in tax money each year." After three years of research, he carefully documents how mismanagement and outdated and unnecessary programs waste our money. In a magazine interview concerning his book, he states:

> What we're talking about are tens of billions of dollars in unnecessary programs which I detail in this book, everywhere from $100,000 a year we spend on the masseurs in the Capitol gymnasiums, to $8 million for a U.S. travel agency, to three-quarters of a billion dollars a year we spend to provide cut-rate groceries for retired military men who are in second career jobs.
>
> This is the kind of waste we're talking about. And if we get rid of that, neither the national welfare nor the national security would be harmed. There would be more money left in the pocketbooks of the American wage earner, and we'd have a little bit more money to put in those programs that are truly necessary.[2]

Mr. Lambro also discussed former President Carter's campaign promise to reduce the number of government agencies from 1,900 to 200.

> When we really boiled it down, you get down to 80 agencies that the Administration says have been abolished. Now, we looked at those 80 agencies and found that . . . the overwhelming majority of them were merged or hidden, if you like, into larger and newly created programs. The only things that have disappeared in the budget are the titles of these agencies. The functions are still being performed. The employees are still there. The program is still there.[3]

There is something about Potomac Fever (or bureaucracy fever) that is catching. Several years ago a young accountant left our church to go to Washington as the administrative assistant to a United States Congressman. During our first visit to Washington, D.C., he showed us around that very important city. After viewing a series of federal buildings, I asked, "How many federal employees are there?" He replied, "Two million." When I naively responded, "Why don't we lay off half of them?" he explained, "Oh, we couldn't do that; it would create a tremendous unemployment problem." I couldn't help thinking, *He has only been here three years, and he's as sick as the rest of them.* Just think what would happen to our economy if we sent 1 million bureaucrats back to their home states to get productive jobs, instead of serving as stifling agents of our nation's economy!

The increase in taxes during the past few years is having a repressive effect on the families, particularly on the average working man who is struggling with the overtaxation that causes him to pay more for taxes than for food and housing. But that isn't the whole story.

Government-Caused Inflation

Everyone knows that inflation is harmful to the family. Who hasn't noticed that double-digit inflation has driven the cost of bread, milk, meat, and everything else out of sight? Recently one of my associates, while studying his utility bill, discovered that although he used 20 percent less fuel than he had in the same month last year, his bill was 80 percent higher. That sounds like a 100 percent increase to me.

Who is to blame for this kind of inflation? The government castigates the Arabs, foreign imports, and the monetary exchange. But anyone familiar with the facts knows that inflation is caused by government. How? Very simple. The government spends more than it takes in; to make up for the deficit, they print more money. The more money they produce and put into circulation, the more they dilute the value of our money. Actually it is just another way of taxing us without labeling it a tax. Because the government cannot resist overspending its income, we face a national debt of over $900 billion. Even though former President Carter promised in 1976 to cut inflation, it rose 6.3 percent in 1977, 8 percent in 1978, 10.2 percent in 1979, and 13.8 percent in 1980, for a grand total of 38.3 percent in just four years.

Whenever I review the causes for inflation, some people conclude, "LaHaye is just a naive preacher; surely the causes of inflation must be much more complex than that—after all, our government says they are." If you won't believe me, consider what David Rockefeller, world-renowned banker and monetary authority, said upon the announcement that he was soon to retire as the head of the Chase Manhattan Bank: "Inflation is a decline in the value of money—and only government has the power to debase the currency by creating too much of it." It may be "politically appealing" to blame "profiteering capitalists" or "greedy workers" for inflation, but it is erroneous. Rockefeller said:

> Over the last decade, one cost has risen faster than food or the cost of housing, faster than wages and infinitely faster than profits. You might think I am speaking of the cost of energy. I am not. The fastest rising cost in the American economy over the past 15 years is neither the cost of haircuts nor mortgages nor any of the other goods and services in the Consumer Price Index (CPI). It is the cost of government—federal, state, and local—paid for through our systematic taxation.[5]

One of the leading reasons that over 60 percent of all married women are working today and 30 percent of the mothers of preschool-age children are in the work force is government-caused inflation and taxation. As severely as inflation affects couples, just imagine what it means to those, like the retired, who are on fixed incomes. It is also disastrous for the single parent.

Ever since the 1940s our country has been courting catastrophe with its introduction of the welfare state. That is, government changed its role from protector of the home to provider for the home. Prior to the 40s, government guaranteed its citizens safety from foreign powers and local hoodlums so the residents could earn their own livings and provide food, shelter, health care, and the other necessities of life for each family member. All that has changed with the welfare state. Now government provides welfare payments, food stamps, medicare, abortion costs, education grants, loans, and so many other federal subsidies that the average citizen has no idea what all of them are. And government has begun to publish pamphlets just to advertise its services.

The high cost of these government services was not so apparent during the 50s and 60s, except by gradual inflation. But during the last decade, our national debt has become so horrendous that we are not only experiencing runaway inflation, but are teetering on the verge of national bankruptcy. When one calls attention to our national debt, most Americans don't take it seriously because, "It's just the government." What they fail to realize is that our national debt is greater than the total debts of all the other countries in the world!

One California state senator echoed the welfare-state mentality during an appropriations bill that cut some fat out of the budget. He lamented, "If we make this cut, we will be unable to care for all the people of our state." My question is, since when has it been government's responsibility to "take care of people"? Forty years of welfare clearly indicate that it is a terribly effective discourager and destroyer of human initiative, self-sufficiency and self-respect.

When my father died, my mother applied for welfare. As we look back, the best thing that happened to us was that we were turned down. Sure it was tough, but it taught our whole family to trust in God and work hard. Government handouts have proved to be a failure. What we need is a rehabilitation program, that is, temporary help granted to an individual who will take advantage of the opportunities available to upgrade his or her skills and become self-reliant. ADC (Aid to Dependent Children) is a national disgrace! All over the country unmarried women are paid for having children out of wedlock, in direct proportion to the number of illegitimate children they have. Relieving people of their personal responsibilities (contrary to Scripture) always proves to be a disastrous social experiment. The waste and corruption of the welfare department is beyond belief, and it creates a constant drain on the finances of the workingman. Dr. E. V. Hill, an outstanding black pastor in South Los Angeles, told me that it takes $32,000 in taxes to give $9,000 to a deserving family on welfare. What happened to the other $23,000? It was eaten up by government bureaucrats.

The Bible says, ". . . If anyone will not work, neither shall he eat" (2 Thessalonians 3:10). Hard work never hurt anyone. In fact, cutting the welfare rolls and forcing able-bodied citizens to work would reduce the crime rate. But when an unskilled worker, by staying home and drawing welfare, can make within twelve dollars a week of what he would earn on a job, many choose welfare—to their own peril.

The Windfall-Profits Tax

The much ballyhooed windfall-profits tax has become another source of aggravation. Advertised as a fifty-cent tax on each dollar profit earned by the oil companies, it sounds like a tax paid by the superrich oil-company giants, doesn't it? Wrong again! You and I are paying that fifty-cent tax in increased prices at the gas pump. The government blames the Arabs for increasing oil prices, but that only disguises the fact that the $70 billion the gas companies will pay in new taxes must first be taken from John Q. Public.

What frightens me is that our legislators relish the $70 billion, and when that is gone, they will look for other windfall profits to charge: auto companies, clothiers, food-stuff companies. Who knows where it will end? The so-called windfall-profits tax could well open a whole new door for government to tax us. Study the chart below, based on broad estimates of taxes now being paid by Mr. Average Worker.

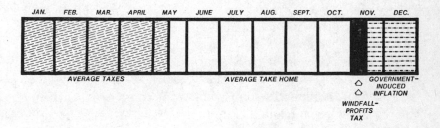

Naturally the accuracy of the above chart will be influenced by amount of income, deductions, number of dependents, charitable contributions, and other factors. But it is easy to determine why so many families are feeling a financial squeeze today. Government, like medical practitioners of centuries gone by, is bleeding the tax-payer's economic life blood. Until enough voters recognize this problem and vote out of office big-spending legislators, replacing them with those committed to cutting its size and cost, government will continue to be the enemy of the family, instead of its friend.

Government Is Out of Hand

President Abraham Lincoln once said that ours was a "government of the people, by the people and for the people." That is no longer true. Today we have a government of elite humanists that is not representative of the people, for they were appointed, not elected, and instead of being "for the people," they are against them—particularly the family.

The size of government today is staggering. Over twice as many people work for government today as lived in the United States at the time of the Revolutionary War. Officially, the federal government employs 3,001,194 people. They are better paid (approximately 28 percent higher than private industry, for the same skills), enjoy a longer vacation time, and are granted better security and retirement benefits, making government an attractive profession, particularly for the security-conscious.[6] But that doesn't tell the full story. When we add the estimated 9 million people who make up Uncle Sam's invisible army of employees, including civilians who work for and are paid by government, plus state and local government employees who are on loan from the federal government, state college and university professors, workers whose salaries are paid largely from taxes, and the military, we discover that the figure of 14 million government employees is not exaggerated. In other words, at least one out of every eight people in America works for some branch of government. Michael Novak and others suggest that the true figure is one out of six. The following chart, designed after a growth study by Morgan Guaranty, provides a historical perspective:

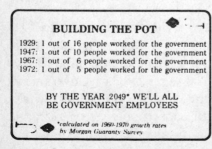

BUILDING THE POT

1929: 1 out of 16 people worked for the government
1947: 1 out of 10 people worked for the government
1967: 1 out of 6 people worked for the government
1972: 1 out of 5 people worked for the government

BY THE YEAR 2049* WE'LL ALL
BE GOVERNMENT EMPLOYEES

*calculated on 1960-1970 growth rates
by Morgan Guaranty Survey

Since government is not productive, adding little or nothing to the gross national product, at least seven people have to work and sacrifice to provide for one government employee. But even this is not the whole story. Businessmen tell me that government employees have created so much paper-work and record keeping for them that they are required to hire one extra employee for every six staff members, just to keep records and fill out forms. Who pays for that extra employee? You do, of course, in higher commodity prices. What most taxpayers forget is that since all these unnecessary government employees have to justify their existence, they create an unbelievable amount of unnecessary and time-consuming paperwork and industrial standards, the cost of which is passed on to the consumer.

> Whirlpool Corporation, of Benton Harbor, Michigan, has re-leased a study showing its cost of meeting government regulations in 1977, beyond costs that would have been incurred for sound busi-ness reasons anyway.
> The cost? $14,619,976 to meet Energy Department rules, $3,156,769 for the Environmental Protection Agency, $1,207,167 for the Occupational Safety & Health Act, $492,308 for the Equal Em-ployment Opportunity Commission, $412,378 for the Federal Trade Commission and $298,733 for the Employee Retirement & Income Security Act.
> The total was $20,187,331—which cost stockholders 22 cents per share in earnings. More than 287,000 man-hours were spent by Whirlpool employees to comply with the regulations and 13,200 pages of documents were sent to the six agencies.
> Whirlpool could have made a lot of washing machines and refrig-erators with the money and manpower spent on paper shuffling.[7]

A *U.S. News & World Report* article on paperwork is equally in-formative:

> In the 12 months ended last September 30 (1978), the General Services Administration, the Government Printing Office and the Bureau of Engraving and Printing bought 330,752 tons of paper for use by federal agencies.
> How much is 330,752 tons? It translates into 66 billion sheets of standard 8½ x 11-inch paper. As such, it would:
> 1. Pave a strip 2,882 feet wide from New York City to Los An-geles.
> 2. Make 48 trips to the moon, which is 238,857 miles from the earth.
> 3. Circle the equator 461 times.
> 4. Cover Washington, D.C., with the blanket 25 sheets thick.
> A single federal form—the Truckers Daily Log, required by the Department of Transportation—generates 1.2 billion sheets of paper annually.[8]

It would help our economy enormously if, during the next decade, we cut 50 percent of these government bureaucrats out of our federal, state, and local payrolls, not just because of the $140 billion that 50 percent would save us, but because of the approximately equal amount of waste and unnecessary activity they generate. Government has become the largest employer in our nation, even though this country is supposed to be committed to free enterprise. Frankly I think it is a tribute to our system that it can carry so much bureaucracy. Can you imagine what our standard of living would be if we could rid ourselves of a significant portion of it? If we do, it will not come without a fight, for, historically, government has never cut its own size; instead, like yeast, it feeds on itself and the people who pay its salary.

The Rising Elite Bureaucracy

Ever since World War II this mushrooming elite ruling class has been increasing, not only in number, but in power and influence. As Novak has pointed out:

> A new class does not often emerge in history. When such a new class emerges, it brings in its train a new politics, a new culture, a new morality. . . . There is in this new class a very strong interest in making itself the center of our culture.[9]

Today this elite class is called government or the bureaucracy. Actually it is a class within a class. Most of the millions of government employees are loyal and faithful American citizens, but for the most part they are kept in the lower echelons of the bureaucracy. The elite ruling class—those who make and administrate the plans, regulations, and policies of government—are predominantly atheistic humanists committed to changing our morals, beliefs, family life, economic system, and ultimately, our government itself. How else can we explain that in the last twenty years almost every law and regulation of our bureaucracy has been harmful to the family?

For example it used to be possible to pray and read the Bible in the public school. Sex education was taught with moral values, but government-sponsored educational programs are antagonistically opposed to morals and have created an unprecedented wave of promiscuity, teenage pregnancy, VD of the worst kind, and suicide among teenagers. Homosexuals are no longer considered perverts but welcome employees in the federal government; legalized abortions have resulted in over 10 million murders of the unborn; and parents, rights are repudiated by our self-appointed elite rulers.

The danger of big government was not lost on Thomas Jefferson, who said, "That government is best which governs least." Nor is it lost on today's average citizen-taxpayer. Consider the unsolicited comments returned in the *Better Homes & Gardens* survey on families: "I am appalled by the bureaucratization of the daily life of American families. We are overpromised and underserved. With paternalistic social programs that take away independence, individuality, and industriousness, our initiative suffers." And from Texas came this demand: "Get government out of our lives. If the government didn't take so much, they wouldn't have to 'help' so much."[10] A woman from Rhode Island complains, "Any programs run by government are awkwardly inefficient, expensive, and wasteful. We need less government, not more."[11]

Seventy-three percent of those who responded indicated that they wanted government out of their lives as much as possible. A family from Michigan wrote:

> Thomas Jefferson listed the acts of tyranny committed by the King of England, and our government leaders should take heed of the tenth item—"He has erected a multitude of new offices and sent hither swarms of officers to harass our people and eat out our substance." The King was a piker compared to the group we've got in Washington.[12]

One interesting report indicated that only 8 percent thought we needed more government-subsidized day-care centers. Why then did the 1981 preliminary WHC report on Children and Youth call for more day-care centers? For two reasons:

1. They are interested in controlling the minds of this next generation's children.
2. They believe in more government, not less.

The average citizen seems to understand that the leading cause of women being forced into the work force is the size and cost of government. As one man put it:

> If the government hadn't given away so much of our hardearned money, made so many government programs, had so many non-productive people tied up in government agencies, a wife wouldn't have to work unless she wanted to. She could be home raising her family, which is the most economical and intelligent way to support family life.[13]

Not only is welfarism causing many mothers to work outside the home against their basic desires and instincts, just to pay for this government form of socialism; it is also having a devastating effect on morality and initiative. Pastors in the ghettos of our country tell me that welfarism is disastrous to the spiritual life of their members. One pastor in Philadelphia protested, "Some of the men in our church can hardly afford to be moral, for if they divorce their wives and live out of the home on weekends, their welfare payments are higher." A Florida pastor noted that social-security payments (planned by government without regard for moral or family virtues) are causing basically good people to live together without marriage because, if they marry, they will lose some of their benefits. A newspaper reporter recently mentioned that a couple who had lived together for three years without marriage decided they would legitimize their relationship, but discovered it would cost them $1,600 a year in additional taxes, so they called their wedding off.

In Seattle and Denver, thousands of people were granted guaranteed incomes and compared carefully to a control group that was not. According to Tom Bethell, Washington correspondent for *Harper's Magazine,* the divorce rate was higher among the welfare workers than among those who had to work for a living. In addition he indicated that welfare tended to demoralize the husband and family head, was inclined to deprive children of their natural respect for their father, and produced an increase in crime. I believe this same frustration that accelerates crime and divorce also fuels the problems of child abuse and battered wives, about which we hear so much today.

537 ELECTED OFFICIALS

* APPOINTED CABINET MEMBERS & FEDERAL JUDGES
APPOINTED BUREAUCRATS

** TOP LEVEL CAREER BUREAUCRATS, DIPLOMATS, etc.
HIGH PERCENTAGE OF HUMANISTS

3 MILLION EMPLOYEES

* These appointments reflect the degree of humanism held by the President who appointed them. The judgeships often outlast the President who appointed them. For example, the New York Times said:

> "By the end of this term, President Carter will have appointed at least 265 federal judges, 40 percent of the entire judiciary. Prof. Sheldon Goldman of the University of Massachusetts tells the New York Times that the Carter appointees are overwhelmingly liberal and their impact on the nation will be felt long after Carter retires to Plains."

** A high percentage of top level bureaucrats are humanists for the simple reason that humanists have long made government service a goal in order to control the American people. Humanists, like Christians, are an invisible brotherhood; consequently, when they meet, they develop friendships and help to elevate each other to high office. They share many common beliefs, dreams and goals, such as the need for establishing a godless, amoral, self-sufficient (autonomous from God) individual who finds his best function in a socialist world. As I pointed out in my book, THE BATTLE FOR THE MIND, humanists believe in Plato's dream of three classes of people – the elite ruling class, the masses, and the military to hold the latter in control. Naturally, these humanists plan to be our "elite" ruling class. That is the implication of the new expression now making the rounds — "our unelected rulers."

The present welfare-state mentality that is so prominent in the minds of too many political and bureaucratic leaders is not only destroying millions of our families, but is ravaging our economy. It is only a matter of time before our government, with its penchant for spending billions a year more than it takes in, will cause a 1930-style Depression or, even worse, a Germany-style inflation. I was in Germany after World War II, when it took a bushel basket full of money to buy a loaf of bread.

What Can We Do?

There are many things we can do while we still have some freedom. We can wake up and arouse our fellow church members to the fact that while we have been faithfully ignoring government during the last fifty years, the humanists have taken it over until they have gained 60 to 70 percent control. We need to elect strong, committed moralists to government. No moralist can be a humanist: The terms are contradictory. We need to pray that in Congress and the Senate, God will raise up about 30 percent more men or women who are aggressively committed to moral values. As a result of the 1980 election, a 15 percent increase could slow the humanists down to a walk. But for that election to have any lasting value, we must follow it with several others that return more liberal humanist politicians to private life.

America: The Crime Capital of the World

The chief purpose of government is to protect its citizens from both foreign and internal attack, so they can be free to earn their own livings. As we have already observed, for the past thirty years government has increasingly assumed the responsibility of caring for many of its citizens, in the process stripping millions of their self-sufficiency, ambition, and self-respect. This has produced a self-indulgence that induces many to steal what they want, rather than urging them to work toward their goals. Consequently crime has zoomed out of sight.

In addition an overwhelming number of liberal humanistic lawyers have become superliberal judges. (It has been my observation that the legal profession could well be the most humanistic of all the professions, followed by education, psychology, journalism, and political science.) That is why there has been such leniency on crime in our courts. Many judges seem far more concerned about "human rights," proper treatment of the criminal, and rehabilitation than they are about the victims of those crimes. Today we hear more about prison reform, parole, and doing away with the death penalty than making our streets and houses safe for law-abiding citizens.

As the humanists in our courts and legislative bodies have changed or twisted our laws, minimizing or negating the penalties for breaking laws that were based on the Judeo-Christian principles of the Bible, they have made a mockery of our judicial system. Today criminals laugh at the system, and even murderers know they will not be severely punished.

Capital punishment is a case in point. The people overwhelmingly favor capital punishment for capital offenses. Four years ago the state of California passed an initiative to the state constitution, reinstating capital punishment for certain offenses. To date, not one murderer has been put to death. Between the liberal judges and our flaming liberal governor, the law of the state has been circumvented, and our streets are rendered unsafe and violent as a result. The humanist inspired cry that "capital punishment is not a deterrent to crime" is as false as humanism itself. The sooner citizens realize that humanism is based on fallacious assumptions (atheism, evolution, amorality, and so on)—profound, attractive, and high-sounding but erroneous theories that always lead to chaos and human heartache—the better off our country will be. The study of logic tells us that when we start out with a wrong premise, we will always reach a false conclusion. Humanism majors in error. Its primary illusion, of course, concerns its view of man. Humanists hold tenaciously to the theory that man is basically good. From Rousseau to Skinner they have based their sociological theories on this false assumption. In order to do so, they have blinded themselves to human history, with its consistent record of man's inhumanity to man. Today the hardworking, law-abiding citizen is forced to subsidize a humanistic court system and humanist-dominated bureaucracy in government, which will not even protect him when he ventures out into the streets in order to work, pay his taxes, and support his family.

As we view the crime waves of the past thirty years, we cannot blame the police, who feel more strongly about the problem than I do. At great personal risk they try to apprehend criminals, but soon lose heart when they find they are released by ACLU (liberal humanist) attorneys faster than the officers can fill out the paperwork.

Humanists have consistently reacted in one way to my book *The Battle for the Mind.* "LaHaye blames atheistic humanism for everything, even crime in our streets." That is exactly right! Study the following crime rates taken from the annually published FBI Uniform Crime Reports, remembering that during the thirty years

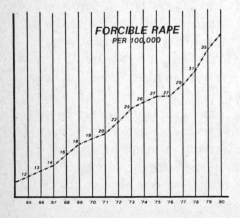

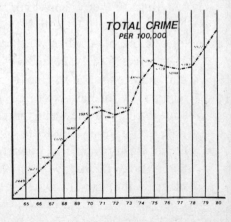

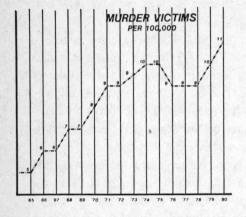

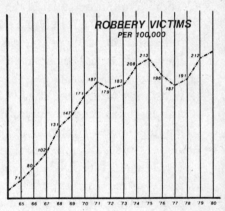

reported here the humanists have exercised a 65 to 80 percent stranglehold on our government, courts, media, and education. Whom else would you blame? The church? We teach obedience to the law and a strict enforcement of the law, commensurate with the crime. When our beliefs served as the policy of our courts and government, America was not the crime capital of the world.

No wonder a recent crime report stated, "Fear of crime is slowly paralyzing American society"—and for good reason. According to the 1979 FBI crime report, "Murders rose by 10 percent, assaults by 10 percent, forcible rapes by 13 percent, and robberies by 12 percent." During the opening months of 1980, "Los Angeles counted 653 homicides for the first eight months of this year, compared with 504 for the same period in 1979—an increase of nearly 30 percent. . . . In Miami, homicides are up to 70 percent over 1979."[14]

How are the liberal humanists in control of our local and federal governments coping with this increasing crime rate? Many are cutting the police force! The reason? Proposition 13 and similar acts by concerned citizens are cutting tax revenues. But since they refuse to reduce welfare and the size and cost of bureaucratic government waste, they cut down on police and fire protection. "In Cleveland, the police force is nearly 1,000 members below its full strength of 2,801, largely because of financial problems."[15] "Detroit, where crime increased 14 percent for the first six months of 1980, nonetheless has begun laying off 690 police officers in a desperate attempt to save the city 27 million dollars."[16] In the last seven years, New York City has reduced its police force by 10,000 officers.[17]

Taxpayers Are Afraid!

For the first time in modern history, American citizens are organizing community crime watches to protect themselves and their property. Thanks to our liberal humanist overlords in government, who have socially engineered this dreadful plight, our people are becoming terrified. The Domestic Bureau's editor for *U.S. News & World Report* wrote, "America is fast becoming a nation living behind dead-bolt locks—with a gun tucked away in a closet."[18]

A survey based on interviews with 1,047 people sponsored by A-T-O, Inc., an Ohio firm which specializes in security systems and similar products, determined that "fear of crime" is forcing Americans to reevaluate their life-styles.

- Four out of every 10 Americans feel that they are vulnerable to murder, rape, robbery or assault in their everyday environment.
- Women and blacks are most afraid of violent crime. Among women, 46 percent are "significantly frightened." For blacks, many of whom live in high-crime slum areas, the figure is 48 percent. . . .
- Fear of crime cuts across all layers of society and geographical boundaries. Fifty-two percent of people in big cities are fearful, compared with 41 percent in small cities, 39 percent in suburbs and 31 percent in rural areas.
- Fifty-two percent of all the people interviewed own guns for personal protection. . . .
- Nine out of 10 Americans now lock their house doors and identify visitors before allowing them to enter. Seven out of 10 keep their car doors locked when riding. Six out of 10 always telephone a friend after a visit to announce their safe arrival home.[19]

For years we never locked our house doors, even in southern California. That day has long passed! During thirty-three years of marriage, my wife and I had never been robbed, until two months ago. While speaking at a women's conference in Memphis, Tennessee, Bev's motel room was broken into, and she lost all the jewelry gifts I had given her during the past four years. Recently we returned from a seminar in Indiana to discover that our house was invaded the night before, relieving us of a few more treasured gifts. Some suggest it was due to our high visibility as a result of our active opposition to anti-moral humanism, but I believe it was the work of professionals, for the security system on our house could only be bypassed in one way, and they found that way.

Whom do we blame for this alarming increase in crime? The

law-abiding Christians or the other hardworking citizens who pay their taxes? The liberal notions that produced this lawless binge didn't originate in the minds of carpenters, plumbers, and working people; they were conceived by the humanist intellectuals in education, law, and sociology. Amazingly they actually think of themselves as intellectuals, ridiculing our "simplistic answers" to the complex problems they have fomented. Until enough citizens awaken to the futility of their dangerous theories and vote the liberal humanist social planners out of government, we will continue to be the crime capital of the world.

The Causes of Crime

Only when a sufficient number of voters understand the real causes of crime will we be able to rescue our nation from its collision course with anarchy and once again establish our homes as havens of safety for our children. Here is my explanation:

1. Our atheistic, anti-moral, humanistic educational system from kindergarten to graduate school has brainwashed millions into thinking that "there are no moral absolutes" and no Supreme Being who will one day hold us accountable for our treatment of our fellowman. Even Will Durant, an acknowledged atheist and our oldest living historian, admitted:

> ... Darwin removed the theological basis of the moral code of Christendom by offering us evolution in place of God as a cause of history. And the moral code that has no fear of God is very shaky. That's the condition we are in. I don't think man is capable yet of managing social order and individual decency without fear of some supernatural being overlooking him and able to punish him.[20]

When asked, "Is religion really necessary to have morality in a society?" he said:

> Historically it seems so. Human beings are not predominantly social. They are predominantly individualistic, and they have to more or less be commanded in their social behavior. In order to control those individualistic desires, every society develops a moral code— Ten Commandments or other forms—controlling the individualistic impulses. And they are indispensable to the continuance of any society.[21]

2. The Protestant work ethic has been destroyed by humanists, who have taught millions of our youth that they are not responsible for their station in life—government or society is. That philosophy strips the individual not only of self-respect, but of self-denial, self-control, and personal ambition, which are required for success in any field. Actually it is not the Protestant work ethic alone that the liberal humanist educators love to ridicule, but the biblical mandates, "Man must earn his bread by the sweat of his face" and "he that doesn't work shouldn't eat." Some readers will remember when our streets and homes were safe and this slogan was popular: "Necessity is the mother of invention." That was before our brilliant humanist overlords convinced the voting public that a government-planned socialist economy was better than free enterprise. Now millions of idle teens grow up never learning to work for what they want, believing that government and society owe them a living. My grandmother's old saying is also discredited by today's liberals: "An idle mind is the devil's workshop." Idle, unchallenged minds are fertile grounds for criminal thoughts. And the greatest crime is often what the humanists have done to the criminal.

3. In the past forty years there has been an increased leniency on crime. As the crime rate soars, bleeding-heart liberal humanist psychiatrists, educators, and judges, still infatuated by the notion that man is basically good, are reducing jail terms at a time when hardened criminals should be kept off the streets until they learn to respect the lives and property of others. Our papers repeatedly carry accounts of psychiatric testimony that encourages judges to declare criminal types sane and fit again for society—at the peril of innocent victims. Our courts should follow a policy of severe penalties for severe crimes. The biblical civil-government mandate "An eye for an eye and a tooth for a tooth" would rapidly cut down the crime rate. Admittedly our humanist social planners go wild with a false sense of humaneness, but isn't it more humane to make a first offender responsible for his deed to the point of working it off in served time or forced labor? Our courts teach all first offenders a lesson: They either pay for their actions or get away with crime. You can be sure that their future actions will be determined by which lesson we teach. We should stop making crime profitable.

4. The abolition of capital punishment is dangerous. No sane human being likes capital punishment! But until our society hears the cries of the increasing number of innocent victims rising from their graves, condemning humanist-inspired error, our courts will not reverse their decisions. According to the biblical principle, "He that taketh man's life—his shall be taken." We will permit more individuals to be murdered by leniency than by a just form of capital punishment. Unfortunately some people have such little regard for human life that they will murder other human beings. We can only deter them by the realistic threat that such action will come at the risk of losing their own.

5. Our courts are faced with interminable delays. A well-advertised crackdown on crime, with speedy and just enactment of sentencing, would reverse crime rates all over the country, for it would make many criminals, particularly the young, think twice about taking someone else's property or life.

6. Free access to drugs has greatly increased crime. Law enforcement officials have a term for it: *drug-related crime.* By that they mean crimes (usually thefts) committed for the purpose of obtaining sufficient money to feed an addict's habit. If the humanists had not been so successful in their demands for so-called freedom of choice and in their distorted application of human rights, we would not have such legal entanglements on law enforcement, giving pushers and dope peddlers freedom to destroy our youth by enabling them to have access to drugs almost everywhere.

7. We are suffering from the results of free access to pornography. The increase in forcible rape can be blamed on a comparable increase in pornography and filthy movies. The last thing a young man during the height of his sex drive needs is to have it stimulated by pornography. Humanist lawyers and judges in and out of the ACLU have done everything they can to strike down all laws against pornography—at the expense of rapists, perverts, sadists, and even more, their victims.

8. Vocational frustration has been caused by our anti-God, antimoral educational system. Today's public schools do a poor job of educating our youth; their methods leave children ill prepared for life, leaving them with little hope for the future and leading many

into criminal activity as their only way out. This value-free humanistic brainwashing in the name of education is a crime itself. It takes
money from taxpayers, 84 percent of whom, according to pollster
George Gallup, "believe the Ten Commandments are valid
today,"[22] and it teaches the philosophy of humanism. This is a sin
against both God and taxpayer.

Crime is much older than humanism. In fact it is as old as man,
for the first child born (Cain) slew the second (Abel), his own
brother. (So much for humanism's touted notion that "man is good
by nature.") Humanism did not cause crime, but its antibiblical
theories have certainly increased it in our country. Crime rises in direct proportion to humanism's influence on a culture. Can you
imagine what America will be like if the humanists reach their objective of making this nation a humanist country "by the year
2000"? We will experience the same chaos and revolution that char-
acterized the French Revolution. Since Voltaire, Rousseau, and
other Age of Enlightenment thinkers were humanists, what humanism did for the families of France, it can do for America—if we sit
back and let it. The ministers of the Moral Majority, Religious
Roundtable, and other pro-moral, profamily groups have declared,
"Over our dead bodies!"

If you believe the newspapers and the speeches of government
bureaucrats (usually prepared for their effect when printed in the
papers), you may conclude that the consistent crime increase each
year is the result of unemployment. While it is true that an unem-
ployed criminal may decide to steal because his pockets are empty,
I cannot imagine why unemployment should cause an increase in
rape, child molestation, violence, and even murder. To be honest,
crime has increased steadily in this country in direct proportion to
the influence of secular humanism on the thinking of our courts,
lawyers, judges, parole boards, and social workers. Most of these
people have ingested massive doses of humanistic philosophy during the pursuit of their degrees. Consequently, during the past fifty
years, these people, with their liberal humanist obsession with individual rights (or as many of them like to label it, human rights),
have overlooked the rights of the victims. We stand idly by as lenient laws are passed; capital punishment is all but abolished; repeat

criminals receive little or no sentences; and early paroles are often granted to dangerous criminals. Unfortunately the liberal humanists in the legal profession are not forced to bear the responsibility for their actions. If the liberal law-school professors, the humanist judges at all levels, and the profiteering lawyers who have so successfully circumvented judges had to pay for their part in putting hardened criminals on the street, where they can commit more crimes against innocent victims, they would take another look at what they have done to our society. I suspect that if 5 percent of their personal incomes were somehow assigned to the victims of the hardened criminals they set free, a more responsible standard would be established to protect the innocent from those who have proved that they have no regard for law, man, morality, or God.

Chief Justice Warren E. Burger, speaking before the American Bar Association in Houston, Texas, in February 1981, suggested that "Lower court judges should start cutting back on the rights of criminals and criminal defendants. The American justice system suffers from too many protections for the accused and too few protections for the victims and potential victims."[23] The chief justice also proposed that more restrictions be placed on the rights of convicted criminals to seek judicial reviews.

To the above suggestions most liberals scream, "Intolerant!" or, "Discrimination!" or even, "Religious bigotry!" In so doing, they are refusing to face the fact that their philosophy is rendering our streets unsafe and causing untold thousands of people to experience needless heartache and loneliness. During 1980 more people were murdered in New York City than in the entire country of Sweden. South American countries have entire revolutions with less loss of life than the United States in an ordinary year.

The latest crime reports out of Washington are frightening. "Each year, one out of every eight American households experiences at least one murder, rape, robbery, assault, or burglary."[24] United States Attorney General William French Smith said, "... fear for personal safety is pervasive among people of this country. From Watts to Beverly Hills and from Washington to Central Park in New York City, most people don't feel safe walking around the block after dark."[25]

An official of the Los Angeles Police Department said that their investigation of 242 drug users with at least a "$100-a-day habit" revealed a combined total of 23,476 crimes. Figure it out: Where is an unemployed drug user going to get $36,500 a year to feed his habit, not including his other living expenses? These figures are awesome when we learn that "about 2,900 persons sought by the Drug Enforcement Administration now are fugitives."[26]

Yet if government cracks down on drug-related criminals or tries to appropriate more money to stop the flow of illegal drugs, who is it who screams? The humanists in the media, government, or the ACLU.

Almost everyone who reads this book knows someone who was senselessly killed or widowed by an experienced criminal. One of my very dear friends goes to bed every night alone and has for five years, because a lenient judge and parole board reduced the sentence of a killer. In the name of humanistic justice we have become a nation of injustice.

I look forward to the day when our streets are safe for children, women, and the elderly. But that will never happen while humanists make and enforce our laws. It may not be much longer, however, until the rising crime rate will inspire politicians to realize that lifetime tenure for judges is an unworkable and unrealistic practice. We need legislation that will limit the term of all judges to eight or ten years. If senators are limited to six years and presidents to four, certainly our judges, who seem to have learned how to impose their standards of lawless law upon entire communities, should have to face reappointment or election, based on their past decisions.

Crime Shouldn't Pay

As a result of the FBIs latest crime report, which highlights the nation's unprecedented crime wave, politicians are beginning to heed the electorate's concerns. In California alone, 130 pieces of legislation have proposed stiffer penalties for the lawless. The following areas arc of particular concern:

1. Repeat offenders should be made to serve out the rest of their first penalty before starting the second.
2. Use of a gun in any crime should always result in a jail term (probably twice what it otherwise would be).
3. No bail should be available for repeat offenders, but a speedy trial should be assured.
4. Higher bail should be set for violent crimes.
5. Penalties for youthful criminals should be the same as those for adults. A beating or shooting by a toughened minor can be just as deadly as by an adult.
6. Plea bargaining may speed the case through the courts, but now there is little similarity between the final sentence and the crime.
7. We must eliminate or drastically reduce the practice of *diminished capacity,* the unsound theory that a criminal should not be held responsible for crimes he committed, when a psychiatrist testifies that he was not responsible at the time or had no real criminal intent. No man alive, including a gifted psychiatrist, knows what was really in the mind of another.
8. All violent criminals should bear the full responsibility for their actions, whether or not they are deemed mentally competent.
9. Stiffer penalties should be instituted for drunk drivers. It is estimated that over 25,000 traffic fatalities per year may be directly attributed to alcohol. All drivers under the influence of alcohol should lose their licenses for one year for a first offense, five years for the second offense, and ten for the third—regardless of whether or not an accident has occurred.

Excessive crime today is the inevitable result of our "soft on crime" policy. We need to return to the old adage, "Crime doesn't pay."

Humanism Causes Crime

The legal profession, with its liberal humanist law schools, and education, with its equally liberal graduate schools, are among the most liberal of all professions. Of all the professions they have done the most to ensnarl our courts, pervert our code of justice, hamper our law-enforcement agencies, and turn many of our metropolitan areas into unsafe welfare city-states. During the past forty years, these two anti-moral fields have exercised an increasing influence on our country, until they control most of our major institutions, except religion.

Humanism always produces chaos. Today our country is the crime capital of the world. As a minister I don't take the blame for this, nor should the millions of people I represent. We can lay the responsibility right at the feet of the humanists. They are the ones who campaigned to do away with the death penalty. They seem more concerned with the rights of criminals than with the rights of their law-abiding victims. They have pushed for early paroles so that criminals can rape, murder, and rob several times during their lifetimes. They are the ones who teach that society should take the blame for criminal behavior.

America was founded on a respect for law and order. However, our great anti-moral humanist social planners have rendered our streets unsafe, jeopardized our very homes, and called that progress. Until we return to the biblical principle that every man shall give an account of himself, we will continue to produce an irresponsible and self-indulgent society that is unwilling to work for what it wants and prefers to steal or kill to get it. That is anarchy! And sometimes I think that humanists actually desire social turmoil in order to foment a revolution—knowing that such disorder is always followed by a dictator or totalitarian regime, and they plan to name their own dictator. Extreme? Check your history! That is exactly how Napoleon Bonaparte came to power after the French Revolution, and it is the same way Lenin took over Russia during the 1917 Revolution.

The only way to avoid such a reign of terror is to elect committed moralists to government office for a sufficiently long period of time to root the humanists out of our governmental bureaucracy—not just on the federal level, but in state and local government as well.

The humanists have set the year 2000 as their goal to "make America a humanist nation." We slowed them a little in 1978, even more in 1980. By 1984 we should have reversed their trends and by 1990–1996 to a large degree nullified their erosive influence on our culture.

Pray that at least 200,000 Christians and pro-moral citizens will run for every elective office in the land (80,000 or more just for school-board members) during the next decade. And ask God that 2 million other Christians (4 percent of the Christian population) will become so concerned about our country that they will volunteer to help candidates by doing precinct work, telephone calling, and many other things necessary to get the right kind of people elected to office. When enough Americans realize how very dangerous humanism is, they will fight it with all their might and will turn this country around. I firmly believe it can be done! That is the reason my wife and I travel over 150,000 miles throughout the country each year, warning everyone who will hear that the enemy is not the Russians or the Chinese; it is the American humanists in government, in education, and in the media.

Once again, I mean them no harm, for they are welcome to live in the free land of America. But it is wrong for them to live off our taxes, make our laws, and educate our young (brainwashing them with humanism). They comprise less than 10 percent of our population, but are currently among the elite ruling class called the bureaucracy. They must be returned to private life.

A friend of mine picked up a member of the Nixon cabinet at the San Diego airport. Knowing that they shared a conservative philosophy, he respectfully pointed out to this high officer of the administration that his friends were disappointed in his performance. Apparently his department was as liberal under a Republican administration as it had been under two successive Democratic presidents. The cabinet member's reply took his old friend by surprise: "I am as disappointed as you are in my ability to turn my department around." He went on to explain that government was not what he thought it would be. Government bureaucracy was so entrenched that he was almost powerless to make many necessary changes. Those with seniority consistently replaced themselves with bureaucrats as committed to liberal humanism as they had been. Even when he forced them to do something, they dragged their feet, delayed implementation, and did as little as possible. "They know I am here for only four or, at best, eight years, whereas they are permanent government employees and will be here long after I'm gone." This country doesn't just need a president and Congress committed to aggressive conservative principles. We need at least twenty-five years of such leaders to rid ourselves of the elite humanist bureaucrats who make up the true Washington establishment.

Our Elite Rulers Are Antifamily

The government's attacks on the family during the past twenty years have become so apparent and frequent that almost everyone recognizes them. (Remember, government is made up of people, yet people in the government are attacking our families!) In fact Sacramento and your state capital are as guilty as Washington in this regard.

My first experience with government meddling in my personal life came at the age of twelve. Congresswoman "Ma" Perkins led the fight to pass the Child Labor Law, which got me fired from my newspaper route because I was "too young" to do that kind of work. My response then is still valid: "Nuts!" I had been selling magazines since I was nine, so work was nothing new, but now my friendly government wouldn't let me help my widowed mother as she slaved in a factory to keep our family together during the decade after the Depression.

Since then I have noticed that almost every law government passes is in one way or another harmful to the family. Exceptions are few and far between. Government increasingly meddles in the affairs of families, so smitten are they with the notion that parents just are not capable of providing for their own children. Some bureaucrats are suggesting that government-controlled preschool day-care centers be compulsory, just as are grades K–12.

The minimum-wage law is another classic example of government mismanagement. Intended to help the poor, it actually hurts young people. An inexperienced youth possibly is not worth $3.25 an hour; thus many companies do not hire young people who could earn $2.50 or so. Consequently, in frustration, these young people run the streets and get into trouble. If government kept its nose out of the problem, many more youth would use their boundless energies productively and learn to work for a living in the process.

Probably the most dangerous piece of legislation came down the pike in North Carolina. Governor Hunt signed into law the Child Health Plan for Raising a New Generation, which established a "second home" for children who are subjected to child abuse by their parents. But it also means that a fourteen-year-old who does not want to live by her parents' moral standards, attend church, or obey their rules can flee to the state-financed health-care home, where she can get outfitted with contraceptives, make arrangements to have an abortion, and be placed in a foster home. That serious invasion of family privacy is the current plan of the humanists who control our government. One humanist let the cat out of the bag when he stated, "We must save this generation of children from their parents."

The Bible says, "Foolishness is bound in the heart of a child . . ." (Proverbs 22:15). God gave children to parents to help them through these stages. Who of us cannot remember going through that foolish and rebellious phase of life? Fortunately we did not have another home to run to, so we learned to conform to our parents' rules.

I am thinking of two fifteen-year-old girls I knew who, at a rebellious stage and at a time of high libido, were so "boy crazy" that they could easily have drifted into a tragic life of immorality. Fortunately they had fathers who fought them every inch of the way. Gradually they rode out that first sexual arousal wave and came to their senses. Today, one is married to a minister and the other is a missionary; both are happily married with children of their own.

Unfortunately the North Carolina plan is a pilot program that may be launched in every state in the Union. I have seen the "Masterplan for California's Children and Youth," and we intend to fight it vigorously, for it preempts the traditional rights of parents and totally ignores the church.

Another of my confrontations with antifamily policies occurred when our eighteen-year-old daughter came home from the doctor's office after her college-entrance physical exam. Slamming her things on the table, she loudly pronounced, "That's the last time I will visit that doctor!" She then related his final conversation. "Lori, I don't know what your morals are, but I want you to know that if you wish me to prescribe contraceptives, I can do it without your parents' consent." I blew up! (Spirit-controlled temperament notwithstanding.) This was an invasion of my family's privacy! When I called my attorney-friend to institute a lawsuit, he quickly informed me that the law is on the doctor's side.

In October 1980 the Utah Supreme Court decreed that a seventeen-year-old girl had the right to choose an abortion, without parental consent. That is only the beginning of the many parental rights usurped by government bureaucrats. During a family seminar in Boston, a lady told the sad story of her sixteen-year-old daughter, who for two and one-half months, was taken from her home by the welfare department, with approval from the courts. Her husband, a Baptist minister, had spanked the girl for an act of rebellion. When she reported it to the welfare department, they took her from the parents and refused to divulge her whereabouts. At first the young rebel liked her newfound freedom in the foster home. After two weeks homesickness engulfed her, but the welfare department still refused to let her see her parents. Finally the girl tricked the caseworker into taking her home for a short visit with her mother. Throwing her arms around her mother's neck, she locked her arms in such a way that the government "social scientist" couldn't break her loose, so she called the judge. He advised, "If she wants to stay home that badly, you can let her." The girl apologized to her parents and admitted that she deserved the spanking. Since when does government have the right to inflict such emotional pain on parents, not to mention a sixteen-year-old girl?

Government-caused horror stories are coming to light all over America, particularly stories of fundamental ministers losing their children to overzealous welfare workers for such crimes as forcing their teenagers to go to church or spanking them. One black minister's fourteen-year-old was transferred to a foster home because the father refused to allow his daughter to attend a dance.

Just the Tip of the Iceberg

Our humanist-controlled government is harmful to the family, not because it is government, but because too many humanists control it. Good government protects the family; a government of humanists exploits it. A thorough treatment of this matter would include such subjects as government-paid abortions; inadequate immigration procedures that permit criminals, homosexuals, and other undesirables to migrate to this country; refusal to let our children pray in school; preschool day-care centers controlled by atheistic humanists, who assault the minds of our children (as the Communists do in Soviet Russia); or the provision of $400 million (in the 1981 budget) to finance the legal costs for homosexuals, lesbians, feminists, welfare recipients, and some drug addicts to sue the government to extract monies in order to advance their causes and personal whims. At the same time veterans, the elderly, IRS-harassed citizens, and some Christian schools have to spend their hard-earned money defending themselves from their own government.[27] All this is in addition to our destructive system of public schools.

I do not like to present only problems. I prefer to offer a workable solution. You may well ask, is there one? Yes, with God's help there is, but only one. We must elect pro-moral, profamily people to office: people who understand that a nation's strength lies not in its military might but in its families. Officials must realize that government should protect the family from outsiders, not try to run the family. That government is best that insures the greatest freedom to its families, so they can become self-determining.

When I think of the way some humanists within our government bureaucracy misuse the awesome power of government by attacking the family, I am reminded of a well-known Christian TV talk-show host I met in the Washington, D.C., airport. While approaching him, I observed that he was leafing through a two-inch-thick legal brief, reminding me of the newspaper report that he had been summoned to Washington to testify on his own behalf. After our greeting, he stated, "I have spent over one million dollars defending myself from my own government." All over America, morally minded families are forced to spend money they can ill afford, defending their right to a family that is free and unmolested by their own government.

Government in and of itself is not evil. Only when evil people can steal into government does it become harmful. I hope Christians' new awakening to their scriptural responsibility to be a part of government as "ministers of God" (Romans 13:1–6) will cause thousands to run for all kinds of public offices. If we don't, the humanists will. And the Bible teaches: "When the righteous are in authority, the people rejoice: but when the wicked beareth rule, the people mourn" (Proverbs 29:2).

Notes

1. "Is Government Helping or Hurting American Families?" *Better Homes & Gardens* 58 (September 1980), p. 19.
2. Richard L. Lesher, "The Story the Networks Don't Tell," *Human Events* 40 (30 August 1980), p. 9.
3. *Ibid.*, p. 9.
4. Judith B. Gardner, "When You Look Beneath Good News on Prices," *U.S. News & World Report* 89 (1 September 1980), p. 30.
5. Donald C. Bauder, "Economist Sees Shift by Rockefeller as Bid for Reagan Cabinet," *San Diego Union*, 15 October 1980.
6. "Profile of Federal Workers," *U.S. News & World Report* 89 (4 August 1980), p. 39.
7. "Truck Hijackers Have Good Reason to be Alarmed," *Los Angeles Times*, 29 July 1979.
8. "Just How Big Is the Federal Government? *U.S. News & World Report* 86 (11 June 1979), p. 57.
9. Michael Novak, "The American Family: An Embattled Institution," *Human Life Review*, 6 (Winter 1980), p. 41.
10. "Is Government Helping or Hurting American Families?" p. 20.
11. *Ibid.*, p. 20.
12. *Ibid.*, p. 23.
13. *Ibid.*, p. 24.
14. "Fear Stalks the Streets," *U.S. News & World Report* 89 (27 October 1980), p. 58.
15. *Ibid.*, p. 58.
16. *Ibid.*, p. 59.
17. *Ibid.*, p. 59.
18. *Ibid.*, p. 60.
19. *Ibid.*, p. 60.

20. Rogers Worthington, "Historian Will Durant: We Are in the Last Stages of Pagan Period," *Daily Californian,* 8 April 1980, p. 5B.
21. *Ibid.*
22. "The Christianity Today–Gallup Poll: An Overview," *Christianity Today,* 21 December 1979, p. 14.
23. "Burger Tells Lawyers: Be Tough on Criminals," *Moral Majority Report,* 16 February 1981, p. 14.
24. Ronald J. Ostrow, "1 of 8 Homes Hit by Crime, Panel Told," *Los Angeles Times,* 17 April 1981.
25. *Ibid.*
26. *Ibid.*
27. In 1980 our Christian school and three others were plaintiffs in a case, defending ourselves, with the assistance of Christian Schools International (ACSI), from the government—at a cost of $200,000.

4

Our Public Schools: Family Enemy Number Three

The public-school system, once the most successful of its kind in the world (when it was based on traditional moral values), has, during the past sixty years, become the third most destructive force

in America, at least where the family is concerned. For families with junior-high, high-school or college-age young people, it is even more harmful than the government. For them, the public school, purportedly their friend, has become a deadly enemy. Nothing creates more discord between parents and children than the humanistic philosophy taught in our nation's schools.

Seventeen years ago I led our church to found Christian High School of San Diego, because I could trace the harmful effects of humanism in my two oldest children. Public education has experienced a downhill slide ever since. A cab driver who picked me up at Kennedy Airport asked, "Are the schools as bad in California as they are here in New York City? My kids are getting no education at all. I'm thinking of moving out West!" Such frustration is heard from coast to coast.

In 1957 the Russians shot up Sputnik and indirectly began the destruction of the American school system. Suddenly we were petrified that Russia's educational system was superior to ours (which turned out to be a fraud). The House and Senate voted federal aid to education as a means of curing our sick schools. As a result, like everything else government gets involved in, the patient has become so much worse that today he is almost dead. The cost of public education is eight times higher than it was, while the quality of education has radically declined. Schools have experienced a 328 percent increase in administrative personnel, while teachers have increased less than 100 percent. But the population in our schools is decreasing. (This is due to the population decrease from 3.6 children per family, in 1957, to 1.6, in 1980; in addition, the Christian-school movement now accounts for 10 percent of all educable children, whereas in 1957 the figure was .5 percent).

Have You Visited High School Lately?

A mother asked me, "Shouldn't we leave our children in public school to be witnesses for Christ?" I responded, "You mean cannon fodder for humanism!" Then I asked, "Have you visited your daughter's high school lately?" Most parents think of high school as it was twenty or thirty years ago. I've got news for you, "It's a new world." After a recent visit to one of our local schools, I reflected on the changes in education, during the past forty years. Consider these contrasting lists of high-school problems.

SCHOOL PROBLEMS IN 1940	SCHOOL PROBLEMS IN 1980
1. Truancy	1. Violence
2. Running in the halls	2. Stealing
3. Talking out in class	3. Forcible rape
4. Unfinished homework	4. Teacher abuse
5. Loitering after school	5. Knives or guns
6. Unreturned library books	6. Vandalism
7. Chewing gum in class	7. Wanton destruction of
8. Talking during study hall	property
9. Broken windows	8. Arson
10. Graffiti on walls	9. Rebellion against authority
	10. Gang warfare and violence

By comparing these lists, one becomes intensely aware of society's deterioration in just forty years. What is the cause? It's very simple: Humanism has taken over our once-great school system and, like everything else it touches, destroyed it.

John Dewey, the twentieth-century high priest of humanism, has had more influence on our public schools than any other person. He was first and foremost a humanist. A founder (and past president) of the American Humanist Association, he was also the author of *Humanist Manifesto I.* Obviously believing that humanism was good for mankind, he decided that the way to transform America into a humanist nation was to gain control of our public schools and train a whole generation of children. He has done just that, and the result has been predictable: schools without learning, graduates without education, and rebels without purpose in life.

It would be impossible for me to detail the devastating harm of humanism's teachings on the 43 million school children who are exposed to it every day. This problem is so bad that I am dedicating my next book in this series entirely to education. Modern public education is the most dangerous single force in a child's life: religiously, sexually, economically, patriotically, and physically.

Let's Hear It for Quality Teachers!

Whenever I speak out against our current public school and education, I always alienate some dedicated, quality-conscious teacher or administrator who is still in the system, trying to salvage whatever good he can. Educators, it has been my experience, are very defensive about their profession, and that is part of the problem. In addition, in few districts can one find school-board members committed to traditional moral values, who are aware of the dangers of humanism and thus hire key administrators who are also aware of the problem. Equally as unfortunate, throughout the country, many quality educators who agree that things are in dire straits are often dominated by humanist administrators who seek to control the minds of our young as well as limit the pro-moral teacher's effectiveness.

In 1978 J. Catherine Conrad made this very revealing statement:

> We must help the God-indoctrinated person realize that morals and ethics are manmade. We must teach him that he must update and discard his outdated, immoral, or evil values, replacing them with rational ones. Let us be participating citizens visible in politics. Let us try out for whatever positions are available. Let us take our place on the school boards and improve education. Let us run for city councils. We need atheist county commissioners. We need non-believers wherever political policy is established which can affect human rights, whether it be in education, housing, medicine, the military or any other area.[1]

No doubt the humanists have been doing this to us for years. It is time we wake up, take advantage of our superior numbers, and elect pro-moralists to our nation's school boards. Only then will our country and its schools return to moral sanity.

Parental Objections to Public Schools

Parents and taxpayers are not unmindful of the critical problems faced by the public schools. Some of the political footballs kicked our way to excuse their failures include busing to achieve racial balance, compulsory education, unmotivated students, broken homes, bilingual education, and pressure groups. But those do not cause

American parents' disenchantment with educators. The real problems can be traced back to the changes that Dewey and his disciples introduced because of their obsession to humanize an entire generation of our youth. These six objectives are only a few that could be introduced as evidence. Please ponder them carefully.

1. *Their Religious Indoctrination*   The Constitution states:

> Congress shall make no law respecting an establishment of religion, or prohibiting the free exercise thereof; or abridging the freedom of speech, or of the press; or the right of the people peaceably to assemble, and to petition the Government for a redress of grievances.

Our forefathers did not want government to establish a religion in this country, as European governments did in creating state churches. But in spite of our commitment to "separation of church and state," we have permitted the government to establish the state religion of humanism in our public schools and exclusively teach its religious beliefs to our children.

Atheism, the basic foundation of humanistic thought, was present in the public schools when I was a boy, but so were other religions, including Christianity. We could have religious assemblies, prayer meetings, and youth Bible clubs; Christian teachers could share their faith openly, without fear of being fired. Atheists could teach atheism, and Christians could teach Christianity in the name of academic freedom.

All that has changed, as you well know. The Bible, prayer, and use of school facilities for church activities have been expelled from school. Now *academic freedom* means that humanists and other atheists are free to teach their atheistic beliefs, but Christians may not teach theirs. Consequently atheism has become the official doctrine of public education.

The bizarre part of this is that our so-called community schools are supposed to reflect the values and beliefs of the families in our community. The Gallup Poll on religion revealed the incredible fact that in spite of thirty years of exclusively atheistic teachings, "94%

of the people still believe in God." This survey also indicated that atheists only comprise 4 percent of our nation. In other words, we must suppress what 94 percent of the population believes and allow the minority to expound its view.

John Steinbacher feels that Ashley Montague summed it up best when he told around 6,000 California school board members:

> "I didn't salute the flag because I don't believe in that kind of God and there is no justice in this country."
>
> He went on to say that every child in America comes to school "insane" at the age of six "because of the American family structure."
>
> Exactly what did he mean by that? Well, the sanity-insanity gambit runs throughout the writings and speeches of the relatively small coterie of Humanists who now control public education.
>
> By their own definition, an insane child is one who believes in everything that has distinguished America over the past 200 years—belief in Christ as God; belief in our Constitution; belief in the founding fathers; belief in moral standards of right and wrong; belief in the concept of sin and belief in just about everything that matters to most people in this land.
>
> On the other hand, a "sane" individual is one who doesn't believe in any of those things, especially one who doesn't believe in the old Biblical notion that man is a fallen creature in need of redemption. Rather the "sane" man is one who is born a neuter creature who can be "changed" through manipulation of his environment.[2]

The religious power of education to make atheists of our children was not lost on the nation's most famous atheist.

> At a convention of atheists in San Francisco, Madalyn Murray O'Hare claimed the climate for atheism has changed since she won her Supreme Court decision. She exulted: "Let's face it, there is no way we could have had an atheist convention 10 years ago. Everything today is much better. Part of the reason is public education."[3]

Both atheism and evolution, two of the official doctrines of humanism, are taught in the public school, in spite of the fact that neither can be scientifically proved. The recent and ill-conceived creation-evolution court case did draw to the attention of the nation the fact that California law requires that evolution be taught as a *theory* (though that is often ignored), demonstrating that it cannot be proved. If it is just a theory or belief, it must be identified as a tenet of faith and eliminated from our schools.

Atheism and evolution taught as fact, contrary to the beliefs of parents, taxpayers, and honest people, isn't all that aggravates parents. Many humanists in the public schools are aggressively anti-Christian. Such missionaries of humanism do not let an opportunity pass to ridicule Christian beliefs. When my daughter did her practice teaching in a local high school last year, she was involved in a course on death and dying. The teacher proceeded to ridicule anyone who believed in "life after death, judgment, heaven, or hell." She authoritatively announced, "When you're dead, you're dead; that's the end." In case you don't recognize it, that is raw religious humanist doctrine! Such teachings undermine a child's faith and put children and parents in religious conflict, which is harmful to the family. Lest you still believe that using the schools for religious humanist indoctrination is not an official function of our educators, consider the following statements by humanist educators:

> I think the most important factor moving us toward a secular society has been the educational factor. Our schools may not teach Johnny to read properly, but the fact that Johnny is in school until he is sixteen tends to lead toward the elimination of religious superstition.[4]

> If education is to meet the current and future needs of our society, humanistic objectives and humanistic thought must operate at the very heart of every school and classroom in the nation.[5]

Humanists never need to raise money for the buildings to teach their religious doctrines. Their churches are called schools, colleges, and universities; and you, Mr. and Mrs. Taxpayer, provide them. How long will you put up with such misuse of your hard-earned money?

2. A Socialist Un-American One-World View   Most Americans are patriotic citizens who love their country. Many fathers and mothers served their country in times of war. Can you imagine the conflict that is generated when a child comes home with the weird idea that

America is an "aggressive, capitalist, imperialist" government, that nationalism is wrong, or that we need to think in world-citizenship terms? You can imagine my reaction when my son announced one day that "Russia helped the courageous people of Poland establish Communism as a form of government after World War II." I was in Europe at the time and knew that at the point of guns, the Russians made the Poles adopt Communism as a government. How about this: "The United States should never have dropped the atomic bomb on Hiroshima." My impressionable young son cooled to that idea when I informed him, "If we hadn't, you probably would not be here, for I was trained on a B-29 flight crew for the invasion of Japan. Estimated loss of American life: one million men!"

You must understand, however, that the humanist has a lifelong romance with Marx, Lenin, Mao, and Castro, because he maintains a socialist one-world view. Has it troubled you that our young often view socialism (which has never successfully upgraded economic life anywhere in the world) as superior to free enterprise? Do you pay the salary of teachers to undermine your child's belief in the one economic system that has done more good for more people than any other in the history of mankind?

3. The Public School's Obsession With Sex Education Probably no subject has created more public outcry against our nation's schools than their obsession to teach sex education to anyone who will listen and to many who would rather not.

I have been fighting radical sex education (that is, too much too soon) since 1966, when I warned the school board in our community, "If you teach this radical sex education without moral values, it will be like pouring gasoline on emotional fires and will increase promiscuity, teenage pregnancy, and VD." Those are the very problems plaguing our schools today. And what is their solution? "More sex education!" That is like asking Jesse James to solve the problems of bank robbery.

All over America, parents have been fighting this course that creates an unnecessary obsession with sex as a physical activity rather than an emotional and spiritual union between two lovers committed to each other for life. Instead of heeding the desires of parents, the autocratic humanist high priests of education force even more explicit materials on our young.

The Sex-Education Assault on California Schools

In April of 1980 the wife of a northern California school-board member sent my wife, as president of Concerned Women for America, a copy of the secret draft of a new radical form of sex education called "Human Sexuality." This concerned woman's husband had opposed the document but was overruled, so she sent it to Bev, who brought it home to me. I read the 164-page manual and could hardly believe it! This manual, designed to train sex-education instructors and financed by HEW at a cost of $175,000, actually advocated a field trip to Planned Parenthood *without parental consent*. It also called for a field trip to the local drugstore so children twelve and over could see where to purchase contraceptives *without parental consent!*

This is a gross governmental intrusion into the sanctity of the home, an invasion of the rights of parents; and we, through our taxes, pay the salaries of these anti-moral, humanist bureaucrats.

Fortunately, during the previous year we had organized Californians for Biblical Morality, a group of 1,000 ministers who share our concern for the moral decline of our state. By alerting them, we launched such a letter-writing campaign to the state school-board members that they called the project off; but rest assured, they will be back, because our unelected elite rulers are determined to destroy the moral values of our youth.

Don't buy the old argument of educators that "If parents taught sex education in the home, we wouldn't have to in the school." The truth is, parents aren't afraid to teach sex education to their children; it's just that parents and teachers are in hopeless disagreement as to how much sex education a child needs. Parents don't want their kindergarten through third-graders to be skilled in drawing male and female genitalia, identified with their proper names, and to be able to describe intercourse, conception, and pregnancy the way the *Human Sexuality* manual advocated. No parent is eager to have his daughter taught that abortion is a live option, when it is really a murderous sin. This public-school controversy will rage until we can either rid our schools of their atheistic, anti-moral religion of humanism, or until parents decide that their children are, after all, the little animals their humanistic educators claim them to be and should become as sexually active as dogs and cats.

Frankly I don't foresee the latter being approved in America. Parents will consistently repudiate such a notion.

4. The Antimoral Teachings of Values Clarification   If you haven't heard of values clarification yet, you will. In various forms, it is the rage in many public schools today. Popularized to teachers by Dr. Sidney Simon and modified to some extent by Dr. Lawrence Kohlberg, it is a cross between group therapy, sensitivity training, and peer-pressure brainwashing. Presented with a hypothetical example that is usually much too advanced for its age level, the class seeks a group decision regarding right and wrong. Can you envision third or sixth graders deciding whether a starving Eskimo tribe should let the grandmother die? or whether sixteen-year-old Alice should get an abortion? or whether juniors should tell their parents they use dope or are sexually active?

The teacher, we must understand, being a humanist, doesn't believe in absolute right and wrong. Consequently he can feel good about a group decision being "right." Typical of humanists, whatever is good for me is "good." The class discusses the moral issue involved and comes to the desired decision, without obvious direction. Frankly such teachers are social-change agents and trained facilitators—conversation guides leading the group to amoral decisions. The change agent, or teacher, whichever you choose to call him, totally disregards the parents' moral values in an attempt to help the *child* think like the group (or as they would put it, "for himself"). As the educator knows, two controlling factors are operative in such a discussion:

1. Peer pressure is overwhelming in junior high
2. A group decision usually reaches the lowest common denominator

Values clarification is a devilishly clever technique for modifying the moral values of an entire generation of children. I wouldn't leave my children in such a school for a single day.

I am not alone in making such a statement. Consider this admonition by Police Chief Kenneth R. Watkins of Montgomery County, Maryland:

> The educational institutions have reinforced the dissonance in the family unit. Neglecting their responsibilities to teach the academic skills and perpetuating the culture of the community, they have set themselves up as the agents of social change and have sought to indoctrinate students into a new social order.[6]

Barbara Morris, author, educator, and mother, makes this telling point:

> COMMENT: A good family can instill values that will withstand any Humanistic thinking. Schools can only build on what families send to these institutions. Whenever many good families send suitable subjects to schools, then Humanistic principles will be able to be overcome.

> RESPONSE: A marvelous example of naive, wishful thinking. Educators like to promote this premise—it gets them off the hook when they start using values-changing techniques. Unfortunately, many conscientious parents really believe that their good efforts are all that is needed to protect their children. But it doesn't matter how good the parental influence is; it doesn't matter how much communication exists; the purpose of the schools is to transform the child from whatever he is, to a Humanist. . . . The constant promotion of peer loyalty to peer values and peer behavior and constant values and behavior modification is very difficult for children to resist and overcome, even when they have been warned about what is being done to them. And after all, children have been told they go to school to learn, and learn they do, but usually not what parents want or expect.[7]

Mrs. Morris concludes, "Parents who really care about what happens to their children will take them out of government schools as quickly as possible."[8]

5. *Violence, Crime, Drugs, Pornography*   Dr. Duane Gish observes, "When I went to school, it was a fight; today it is a riot." In many of our schools, discipline and authority are so poor that attending school can be dangerous to one's health. Some of our inner-city schools are so intimidating that young people can only go to the rest rooms in groups of three or more, and some children are so terrified that they don't visit a rest room all day long.

We were shocked to read that high-school girls in Los Angeles, angry over low grades, tossed lighted matches at their teacher, setting her hair on fire. The teacher, who received no support from her principal, later suffered an emotional collapse.

A New Orleans teacher watched two boys throw a smaller child off a second-floor balcony, afraid to interfere lest the boys should turn on her. The National Institute of Education estimates that 5,200 junior-high and high-school teachers are attacked every month; 282,000 students are assaulted, and 112,000 robberies are committed.

Talk about "reaping what you sow," that is what the humanists have brought to our schools. They have spawned permissiveness, self-indulgence, and a self-pleasing, do-your-own-thing atmosphere that is not conducive to learning. Students excel at rudeness, selfishness, and sloth. It is no wonder that learning proficiency has dropped so low.

What Can We Do?

1. As a parent, you must first withdraw your children from these humanist indoctrination centers and send them to a Christian school, if there is one in your community. If not, repeatedly urge your pastor to start one. Four new Christian schools are opened daily in this country. Churches should begin Christian schools, and Christians should send their children to them. Churches must fulfill the God-given mandate to teach their children; furthermore, they have the message, the facilities, and the means to recruit dedicated and motivated teachers in order to produce a quality educational institution.

2. Every large church should add to its staff a qualified and experienced Christian-school superintendent for each well-populated county, in order to help other churches strategically start various levels of Christian schools. Many small churches that could never begin their own Christian schools can provide one or more classrooms in a well-planned school system. Churches should invest in this kind of qualified leadership, not for the building of their own churches, but as missionary projects for their counties. Proper coordination and leadership will avoid duplication. Every church ought to originate a Christian school or help those who have one.

3. Elect to public office Christians or pro-Christian moralists who have the strength of character to oppose humanistic policies. That is particularly true of the 16,000 school boards. If every church in the country would get one of its qualified members elected to the school board, we could turn public education around in ten years. Besides, we would then have 80,000 key people with local name identification to run for higher office.

4. Christian and other dedicated public-school teachers and administrators should be more assertive and aggressive in taking advantage of their position in teaching traditional American pro-family morality. The humanists do not own the public schools! Schools belong to taxpayers, but we have surrendered control to the amoral humanists. We need to oppose evil teaching and counteract humanism with the principles of character building like those upon which the schools were originally founded.

5. Seminars, conferences, and rallies should be conducted throughout the country, to acquaint dedicated teachers with their rights under the law, enabling them to advocate honesty, integrity, patriotism, and morality in the classroom.

6. Elect congressmen and senators who will vote to get the federal government *out* of the public schools. (Test scores have dropped in direct proportion to federal control of education.)

7. Start fundamental/alternative public schools for those students and nonreligious parents who want their young to get an education that provides real skills and character building.

8. Watch the public schools carefully and protest every encroachment of parents' rights; challenge teachings that undermine traditional moral values.

9. Pray earnestly! (2 Chronicles 7:14). Pray for ways to have this humanistic religion and teaching expelled from the public schools. Then our nation's students can go back to getting an education.

This all may sound like an incredibly difficult task for some dedicated people, and you are right. But it is worth it all, to regain our children, families, culture, and country! This is a free country, with an extraordinarily fair electoral process. A growing mood of disenchantment with public education tells us that the wrong people are running our schools. We have watched as phonics were replaced by "progressive education," and now Johnny can't read. The "new math" supplanted hard-work rote learning; and now Johnny can't add, subtract, or multiply. Discipline, punishment, and respect for authority were discarded as old-fashioned; and now Johnny just bums around, smoking pot and popping pills as his learning curve drops to an all-time low. The only notable increases are the billions of dollars spent on education, crime, sexual activity, VD, abortion, and rape. Our schools have turned into zoos, and who is to blame? The mastermind humanists who forsook the proven methods that once made ours the greatest system of education in the world. While we still have our freedom, we should use it to preserve the minds of our young by keeping them out of the reach of the atheistic, humanist educators who serve as missionaries of the most dangerous religion in the world.

The time is ripe for action. Recently I received a call from Senator Hayakawa's office, inviting me to meet with some other pastors in southern California. The purpose for the meeting, according to his aide? "Senator Hayakawa is deeply concerned that our public schools have produced a whole generation of young people without moral values," and he wanted our suggestions and solutions. That is exciting. Evidently he heard the cries of America's moral majority on November 4, 1980. Although he was the president of a humanistic college before being elected to the Senate, he now realizes that humanism doesn't have the answer to mankind's great needs.[9] I hope millions more will recognize that fact.

Notes

1. J. Catherine Conrad, *Humanist of the Southwest,* 1978.
2. John Steinbacher, "To Capture a Nation—Change the Religion," *The American Mercury* 108 (Summer 1972), p. 56.
3. "Atheists Proclaim Their Morality," *The Catholic Review,* 12 May 1978.
4. Paul Blanshard, "Three Cheers for Our Secular State," *The Humanist* 36 (March/April 1976), p. 17.
5. Arthur W. Combs, "Humanism, Education, and the Future," *Educational Leadership* 35 (January 1978), p. 303.
6. Thomas Love, "Police Chief Cites Women's Lib in Youth Crime," *Washington Star,* 23 June 1975.
7. Barbara Morris, *Change Agents in the Schools* (Ellicott City, Md.: The Barbara M. Morris Report, 1979), p. 247.
8. *Ibid.,* p. 249.
9. If you are a public school teacher or administrator who recognizes that humanism is destroying your profession and wish to be contacted when an organization is formed to implement some of the actions suggested in this chapter, write to Commission on Quality Education, 2100 Greenfield Drive, El Cajon, CA 92021.

5

TV: The Electronic Tranquilizer

Television is the most powerful vehicle ever invented to assault the human mind, for it combines both the visual and the aural in

communicating its message. Early in my career as a preacher I learned that people forget 90 percent of what they hear. I found that very discouraging, so I developed the practice of using an overhead projector, because we remember 60 percent of what we see. More recently educators have suggested that we understand 20 percent of what we hear but 80 percent of what we see. A combination of hearing and seeing clearly improves both comprehension and retention.

In just thirty years we have moved from no TV viewers to an entire nation that has access to the "tube." It is estimated that over 100 million people followed the presidential debates. According to a Nielsen survey:

> Children under five watch an average of 23.5 hours of TV a week. Today's typical high-school graduate has logged at least 15,000 hours before the screen—more time than he has spent on any other activity except sleep. At present levels of advertising and mayhem, he will have been exposed to 350,000 commercials and vicariously participated in 18,000 killings. The conclusion is inescapable: after parents, television has become perhaps the most potent influence on beliefs, attitudes, values and behavior of the young.[1]

According to Dr. James P. Comer, associate dean of Yale University Medical School:

> All authority figures have less influence today than in the past—ministers, teachers, policemen and parents. People are exposed to TV much more than they are to church, school or family. Television is a model and people use it as a model for their behavior. . . . And often TV is a bad model. It doesn't promote desirable social behavior. Its only purpose is to get your attention and entertain. . . .[2]

Psychologist Dr. Victor B. Cline of the University of Utah says young and old are similarly affected by TV. "Both adults and young people turn to television to learn what society considers appropriate behavior—as they once turned to the family, the community or the church for guidance," he observes. "There is a tremendous amount of modeling of behavior on TV. . . . Some soap operas . . . are pretty sick in presenting conflict in male-female relationships—deception and lying and double-dealing. The woman who sits glued to her TV set all day and gets this garbage in her brain will be affected in her feelings about her marriage and her relationship with her husband."[3]

It is frightening to realize that TV has more influence on the minds of today's youth than their parents, minister, or church. But as Dr. James P. Comer affirmed, "Authority figures once had tremendous respect and power and influence over people's behavior. Today, in their absence, there is TV."[4]

Such a statement is alarming because the people who control TV are the same ones who have dominated the movies from the 20s to the present, and everyone knows that their lust for X-rated sexuality, violence, and sadism reflects a standard of morals below the bottomless pit. Yet they have access to the homes, hearts, and minds of America's families.

TV Produces Violence

Liberal humanists protest vigorously when I point out that they are responsible for our terribly unsafe cities, yet it is true. One reason (among several) is that the amoral humanists control the networks, the leading TV shows, writers, producers, and many actors. As one writer put it:

> A teenager with a rifle fires at several cars on a busy freeway, spraying their occupants with glass and injuring two people. Police note that a television program shown the night before depicted a similar sniping incident. Crime statistics prompt an Australian author to write a book titled "Murder USA." The specific inspiration comes from a report that murders total 486 during a single year in Philadelphia, a city of two million. Toronto, Canada, the author remembers, has a comparable population but a murder rate of only 41.
>
> In Los Angeles, Calif., the county coroner reports his office is running two days behind schedule in autopsies at midyear because of an unprecedented wave of killings. He expects murders to top 2,000 this year. Ten years ago, there were only 1,500 murders in the entire state.[5]

Dr. Clate Risley was my friend. One night this faithful husband, father, minister, and director of the National Sunday School Association was brutally stabbed on the street, enroute from his office to his home. Only God knows the lonely days and nights experienced by his wife and children because of someone else's brutality, and who knows how much responsibility for his unnecessary death and that of thousands of others across the United States was inspired by TV? Since it refuses to police itself, TV must be brought into control by the people of this country. Obviously the efforts of the courts and our government have been ineffective.

The TV Assault on Morality

Shortly before his death, singer Bing Crosby deplored the "prurient material" often presented on TV. "Its effect can't be anything else but harmful [to children]," he said. "They see these chic, sophisticated people behaving immorally, salaciously. People living together without the benefit of marriage must be the thing to do, they think."[6]

Dr. Jerome L. Singer of Yale University reported the results of a TV study indicating that "attitudes pertaining to any moral value or precept can be altered. And much TV programming is of a type to make it happen, particularly with respect to sexual morality."[7] That, my friend, is what the anti-moral humanists of our TV networks are after: the altering of our moral values.

As I pointed out in *Battle for the Mind,* the traditional moral values of America are based on the Judeo-Christian concepts of the Bible. Liberalism's assault on morality is based on humanism that is out of step with the consensus thinking of America. Even after thirty years of anti-moral programming, our viewpoint is still held by 84 percent of the American people, according to the Gallup Poll; but TV does not reflect that. In the past few years, why has TV programming descended from filth, smut, and innuendo to depravity? Because the humanists who control the industry are out to destroy (they call it "alter") the moral fiber of our country, without which the traditional family cannot exist.

When TV first appeared in the 50s, it was entertaining. Soon it became the chief baby-sitter in millions of families throughout the nation. When the power to communicate their anti-moral ideology was placed in the hands of its current owners, gradually the moral tone began to decline. First, infidelity and premarital sex as accepted patterns of behavior began to appear in programming, suggesting that everyone is doing it. Today material that is an insult to decent people and a negative influence upon our youth is common fare. In fact, comedy has been utilized as a very effective vehicle for ridiculing those who oppose homosexuality, lesbianism, wife-swapping, and other forms of adultery. One program even went out of its way to introduce incest with religious overtones. Bedroom scenes are so vivid and explicit that little is left to the imagination, and yet the producers of such programs complain of the restraints still imposed on the TV industry.

Using the First Amendment guarantee of free speech as a cloak for its immoral programming, TV consistently exalts the anti-moral while ridiculing the moral. While on vacation I saw three ads promoting a situation comedy of four young women living together, agonizing over whether the only virgin in the group should go away to Las Vegas for a weekend with a young man. Although they admitted that "being a virgin is nothing to be ashamed of," they ridiculed her and made her look like a fool. As a viewer, I could come to one conclusion: Only idiots wait until marriage.

Objections to this kind of programming do not come solely from ministers. Consider this article by Ron Aldridge, TV critic of the *Chicago Tribune*, as he comments on "The Women's Room," a vicious attack on marriage, morals, and the family. In fact, it may be ABC's all-time low in degradation programming. Be sure of this: Unless curtailed by government standards of decency, TV shows will get worse.

LOS ANGELES—ABC, the network that gave the world the miniseries, is about to launch yet another programming innovation, this one an assaultive form of video best described as advocacy entertainment.

Like advocacy journalism, it attempts to persuade the consumer to accept a particular point of view. It is admittedly one-sided and blatantly unfair. It is perhaps the most dangerous television trend in the history of the medium.

The vehicle for launching this prime-time madness is "The Women's Room," a three hour made-for-TV film based on the Marilyn French novel by the same title. As television, it is stripped of all depth and insight that may have been present in the book. What remains for the viewing public is a ruthlessly cynical attack on traditional marriage in America, male-female relationships, and much of family life. Males bear the brunt of the assault.

Brandan Stoddard, president of ABC Motion Pictures, admits the film is advocacy entertainment, but he, as do the producers and star Lee Remick, claims it simply advocates choice. Not true, "Women's Room" advocates a particular choice, which is something quite different.

Specifically, the film is a piece of propaganda that commands women to choose careers outside the home, to avoid suburbia at all costs, to even reject much of motherhood. It excludes all arguments to the contrary as it paints a dreary picture of life in the mainstream. If there is any fun, decency, and fulfillment in the traditional American family, this movie ignores it.

It does not, however, ignore the indecencies. Mira, played by Remick, is savaged by men, ravaged by motherhood, and mauled by marriage as she is ultimately driven from the suburban world she entered as the wife of a doctor. . . .

It is a vicious, vicious television program, the likes of which I've never seen before. The producers claim, somewhat proudly, that they want it to make you angry, to make men in particular stop and think. They succeed on the former, fail on the latter.

The film is so obviously distorted, twisted, and unfair that the very people who most need educating about feminist issues will be totally turned off. . . .

Granted, television programs have always conveyed certain values, many of them supportive of traditional family lifestyles. What's disturbingly different about "Women's Room" is that it carries the value-conveying practice to an extreme, to a new degree. It is admittedly an advocate, from network to producer to star. Implicit is the notion that network power brokers have a right to propagandize in prime time, that there is no need to even attempt fairness and balance.

That simply won't do. The laws governing broadcasting quite properly demand that the handful of people licensed to use the public's limited airwaves must, in exchange, be fair and balanced in their news coverage. So should it be with entertainment, which can be an even more powerfully persuasive video form. You may agree with the particular point of view advocated by "Women's Room," but how will you feel if a producer someday advocates say, anti-Semitism under the guise of entertainment? . . .

"The Women's Room" originally was offered to NBC, but the network wisely rejected what the producers had in mind. ABC, a slipping outfit with occasionally slipping standards, should have done the same.[8]

If I had time and space, I could make a lengthy inventory of the pornographic indoctrination now masquerading as TV entertainment. Just turning off the TV set is not the whole answer. The airways are controlled by a government that is supposed to be "of the people and for the people." Such TV programming does not ingratiate itself to the decent people who make up the majority in this country! Besides, we pay for TV. We purchase our sets, we pay extra for the products of the advertisers who buy the time, and therefore we should be served by TV, not mastered by it.

It is wrong when a free country's TV airwaves, which broadcast to 225 million citizens, are controlled by about 100 people who are amoral, humanistic perverts, hedonists, or at best, naive executives, producers, scriptwriters, gagwriters, actors, comics, and other so-called artists. It's bad enough when such degrading entertainment is offered in the theaters of the country, but at least then each individual pays his money because he chooses to attend. It is a national disgrace when such anti-moral programs as "Soap," "Three's Company," "Dallas," "Saturday Night Live," "The Newlywed Game," "The Dating Game," and "Three's a Crowd" are allowed by government to air during prime time. In the order listed, the above were found to be TV's most morally offensive programs in a survey of 420,000 people taken by the Joelton Church of Christ, Joelton, Tennessee. They and other groups, including the Moral Majority and Concerned Women for America, are leading the nation in long-overdue letter-writing campaigns and boycotts of advertisers, in an attempt to clean up TV.

Personally I think letters of commendation to the advertisers of good programming are also appropriate. I have in my files a handwritten letter from Mr. Ray Kroc, owner of McDonald's, thanking me for a letter that commended him for his wholesome, profamily ads. In it he said, "McDonald's will always keep the family image in spite of the more sensational even if we have to be alone." We need more Ray Krocs in American business.

I am convinced that if one TV network were purchased by profamily promoral directors who fired the people now designing the perverted attacks on America's morals and replaced them with those committed to wholesome programming—that which exalts the family, motherhood, virtue, and normal sex roles—the other networks' ratings would drop into limbo. The success of "Little House on the Prairie" ought to teach us that the American people do not prefer the current corrupt programming. One would think that a decline in viewers that matches a decline in morals ought to teach all the networks something. Their refusal to change proves that their first objective is not making money; it is the indoctrination of anti-moral humanism.

Except for Monday-night football and news, I am not much of a TV bug. I do, however, watch "The Today Show" in the morning, during my exercising period (that helps make it less painful) or breakfast. Quite frequently, the program hosts antifamily, feminist, and sometimes anti-moral guests, allowing them to parrot the usual network line. One interview was of an unmarried woman with herpes simplex who had safely given birth to a child—a process that I understand is difficult and takes special medical care to avoid transmitting that most dangerous strain of venereal disease to the offspring. I did not object to her doctor's medical warning, but I vigorously objected to the valueless way this woman was offered national TV time to exalt her immoral life-style. Just like sex educators in our public schools, these stars of national TV did nothing to correct the notion that the joys of premarital sex are worth the risk of a dangerous, incurable form of VD. That is a betrayal of public trust! No mention was made that virtue and morality are still the best preventive of VD. Nor do we hear of surveys showing that couples who practice self-control before marriage enjoy a higher sexual satisfaction level and lower divorce rate after marriage than do the promiscuous.

One guest on a nationally infamous talk show was a mindless psychiatrist who actually advocated that parents encourage their children to use their homes to practice sexual activity. Such hedonistic reasoning should not be dignified by giving it space on public TV, particularly when there is a concerted effort to keep pro-moral programming to the minimum and when those with moral perspectives are frequently ridiculed. The excuse that "we are objective" clearly does not apply when traditional moral values surface.

TV talk shows are powerful sources of antifamily indoctrination. One reason I opposed the Equal Rights Amendment so vigorously was because it would have been devastatingly harmful to the family. Another is that women would have been subject to the draft. Phil Donahue loves to use his popular program to promote his ideals; and Phil was vigorously in favor of ERA, even to leading a parade on its behalf in Chicago. Most of his guests were pro-ERA. Occasionally he would throw a sop to the fairness doctrine by inviting a Stop-ERA advocate. One Miami show pitted attractive and articulate Kathy Teague against former Congresswoman Bella Abzug, a woman air force sergeant, Phil, and the hostile audience made up largely of Bella's friends. Although Kathy held her own against those overwhelming odds, the program insinuated that she represented a handful of old-fashioned thinkers, whereas all surveys clearly indicate that the overwhelming majority of people in this country do *not* want their girls to be drafted or to enter the military.

TV Is Anti-Christian

TV is not only blatantly anti-moral and antifamily but extremely anti-Christian. Except for the religious time so begrudgingly sold to Christian broadcasters (for which they are forced to raise enormous amounts of money, which often draws the criticism of the humanists in the industry, who get paid for presenting their amoral point of view), Christianity is either ridiculed, misrepresented, or ignored. For example, when did you last see a documentary on church growth in America? That subject happens to be the sociological and religious phenomenon of the past three decades, yet it is not newsworthy! We have grown from a small minority to in excess of 20 percent of the American population and, at the rate we are growing, will operate half the schools and total over half the population by the year 2000. Yet TV pretends we do not exist or treats us as the hysterical "religious right." Right of whom? Right of the elite minority who control our TV networks.

Kevin Perrotta, who has done a great deal of research on this subject, reports:

> Television, like the other mass media, views the world without Christian coordinates. That media world of fact and fiction considers right and wrong in humanistic terms, never in terms of God's authority to set standards and to reward and punish. It defines freedom in material and political terms, rather than as liberty from the dominion of sin and evil. It insists on knowing only the natural world, and on ignoring the supernatural.

In the television world, divine providence and faith in God are simply aspects of some people's religion, rather than fundamental dynamics of human life. On television, truth is absolute only for those who think it so; but belief in human progress, individualism, and democratic political methods are hidden absolutes.

Many Christians spend many hours every week looking at such views of the world. This heavy television viewing dulls their ability to see the world from the Christian perspective. . . .

The conflict between world views becomes clearest when television looks directly at Christianity (I am referring to secular programs, not "religious" ones). News programs view Christianity through the lens of secular presuppositions; for example, reporters see the church in terms of traditional versus progressive—hardly a scriptural perspective.

But if television journalism's approach to religious news is misguided, television entertainment's portrayal of Christians and Christianity is downright libelous. Most Christians portrayed on television fall into one of three types: The gentle, slightly muddled, and highly ineffectual preacher (Fr. Mulcahey, the Catholic chaplain in "M*A*S*H," was once stunned when one of his prayers actually "worked" and a sick patient recovered).

*The fast-talking, Bible-thumping, and probably money-grubbing, Elmer Gantry type of evangelist.

*The spaced-out cult member (an episode of "The Rockford Files" portrayed a young woman's rather ridiculous journey through the world of Rolfing, Primal Scream, est, and the local ashram, until she reached what the producers evidently thought was her logical destination: passing out tracts on a street corner). One shudders to think how common this motif may become in the wake of Jonestown.

The first model is nice, perhaps, but scarcely challenging; the second, ridiculous; the third, vicious.

The world of television is a world in which Christians are either dimwitted, dishonest, or dangerous. If one is taking his cues from television, a Christian is not something he is likely to want to be.

In point of fact, television rarely portrays genuine Christianity at all, merely its own smug, snickering, and wildly erroneous stereotypes. Seeing is believing (alas).[9]

The anti-Christian bias of the network moguls should not surprise us. Humanism only perpetuates one obsessive hatred: Christianity. Just as humanists have excluded us from public education or the use of their buildings (although they accept our taxes to fund their religious ideology in school), they have excluded us from TV whenever possible.

Until a complete Christian or profamily TV network can be established, Christians need to protect their families from the anti-Christian programs on the tube by controlling what their children watch.

TV Hinders Education

One educator called TV "the most underused educational tool ever invented." He forgot to add that TV often becomes a substitute for learning. Whether or not we like to face it, education is hard work. One cannot learn to read, write, and do mathematics (the three basics of modern education) without time and effort. TV attempts to replace diligence and energy with fun and games. Susan Sontag, essayist and novelist interviewed by *U.S. News & World Report*, suggests:

> Young people today are less literate than a decade ago. They seem to have less intellectual energy. Television must have a lot to do with it. I have a suspicion that it really changes the way people pay attention and, in effect, damages powers of concentration.
>
> People may have a different way of using their minds as a result of watching television. It's almost like a neurological retraining: If you watch television all the time, it is in some very profound way incompatible with reading.[10]

According to an Associated Press study on a survey coming out of Sacramento:

> ... the more a student watches television, the worse he does in school. California Schools Superintendent Wilson Riles said Thursday that no matter how much homework the students did, how intelligent they were or how much money their parents made, the relationship between television and test scores was practically identical.
>
> Riles concluded that for educational purposes, television "is not an asset and it ought to be turned off...."
>
> More than 500,000 California public school students in the sixth and 12th grades who took tests in reading, language use and arithmetic last year also revealed how much television they watched.

Riles said the results "do not necessarily prove that television watching is a direct cause of lower test scores," but "there are strong statistical relationships."

For example, among 12th-graders, 29.8 percent said they watched zero to one hours of television a day, and they averaged more than 72 percent correct on the mathematics test. The score declined steadily for each hour watched, with those who watched six hours or more, 5.5 percent of the total, averaging 58 percent correct.

Sixth graders declined somewhat less for the first four hours of viewing a day. But the dropoff was steeper beyond the fourth hour—for example, from 65 percent to just over 60 percent correct on the test of written language use for the 20 percent who said they watched more than four hours a day....

"The verbal dialogue that goes on in many of those [commonly watched] programs is of very low quality and the educational value would be nil," Riles said.[11]

One does not have to think for himself when watching TV, and that is one of its chief dangers: Someone else is doing the thinking. Can we *really* trust TV's current programmers to do our thinking for us?

TV Is a Thief of Time and Family Life

Time spent communicating with one another is absolutely essential to good family life. But TV watching robs some of the best hours for that valued communication. One research psychologist, Urie Bronfenbrenner, has expressed this rather poetically:

Like the sorcerer of old, the television set casts its magic spell, freezing speech and action, turning the living into silent statues so long as the enchantment lasts. The primary danger of the television screen lies not so much in the behavior it produces—although there is danger there—as in the behavior it prevents: the talks, the games, the family festivities and arguments through which much of the child's learning takes place and through which his character is formed. Turning on the television set can turn off the process that transforms children into people.[12]

Perrotta wisely points out:

Christians should be particularly concerned about television's interposition between parents and children. We have the responsibility to train our children in knowledge of God, in his character, in obedience to his laws. We carry out that duty most effectively in the natural course of things—eating together, running errands, working around the house, traveling, playing, visiting with friends. Television competes with this process of natural instruction. While children are watching television they are not receiving training from us. They are not gaining experience in obeying their parents, relating to their peers, serving people, or anything else.

Parents who, consciously or unconsciously, use television to withdraw from active child rearing will likely suffer the consequences. Children who are not disciplined properly grow more wilful and harder to handle with every passing year. Parents who substitute television for training can expect that their children will grow more rebellious and less disciplined. Television may be an effective narcotic for undisciplined children; but the temporary peace brought by television may have long-range side effects as children grow less compliant and parents less confident to deal with them.[13]

Some people have the capacity to watch TV and accomplish tasks at the same time. Many of us cannot. A long time ago I concluded that either TV controls me or I control it. Therefore, except for a few sporting events and news programs, it occupies very little space in my family's life. People who spend time watching TV have less time for God, spouse, family, neighbors, and friends. Since most programs are mindless anti-moral fantasy, why bother?

Notes

1. Jerry Rubin, *Growing Up at 37* (New York: Warner Books, 1976), p. 18.
2. Dick Robinson, "TV More Powerful Than Church, Family, or School," *National Enquirer.*
3. *Ibid.*
4. *Ibid.*
5. Jim Cox, "Cable TV Magnifies Moral Debate," *Life's Answer,* October, 1980, p. 88.
6. *Ibid.*
7. *Ibid.*
8. "ABC to Air Vicious Attack on Marriage, Family Life," *National Federation for Decency,* August 1980, pp. 1–2.
9. Kevin Perrotta, "Watching While Life Goes By," *Christianity Today,* 24 (18 April 1980), pp. 18–19.

10. Susan Sontag, "Young People Have Less Intellectual Energy," *U.S. News & World Report* 87 (9 July 1979), p. 69.
11. "Students' Scores Reflect TV Habits," *Globe–Democrat*, 8–9 November 1980.
12. Perrotta, p. 17.
13. *Ibid.*

6

Media: Free or Controlled?

Americans pride themselves on freedom of speech and freedom of the press. In fact, most citizens have been assured that we enjoy a free press and free news-gathering service, whereas in reality our most powerful media (TV, newspapers, radio, magazines, and books) are largely controlled by anti-Christian, anti-moral, anti-free-enterprise and prohumanist influences.

When I say "largely controlled by humanists," I do not mean to indict everyone in the media business as a humanist, for I have met a number of very dedicated Christians in TV studios and at newspaper offices. Recently, for instance, I spent time with a fine Christian brother who manages a radio station in Oklahoma City. But such exceptions, few in number, are usually limited to local media. We find *very few* conservative Christians in the upper echelons of the national media. In addition, many in the media adopt the humanist viewpoint and either purposely or inadvertently advance its goals. They are the brainwashed victims of public education, because they have only been exposed to the liberal point of view.

Humanists Control the Media

To understand what I am saying, keep in mind the five major points of humanistic ideology. As detailed in *The Battle for the Mind,* on the next page are the five basics of humanism (read from the bottom up).

I do not know a national news commentator, TV personality, or network official whose selection of the news to be reported or whose interpretation of the news does not reveal a commitment to at least points three through five of the preceding diagram, even though they are drastically out of step with the majority of the American people.

The great conservative landslide victory in the election of 1980 provides a classic illustration. During the primaries, 320 of the leading newspaper editors and reporters met in Washington, D.C. A straw poll was taken to see whom they favored for president of the United States. The following chart reflects the results:

109 John Anderson	
69 Teddy Kennedy	HUMANISTIC IN PHILOSOPHY
57 President Jimmy Carter	
31 George Bush	HUMANIZED MODERATES
24 Howard Baker	
20 Ronald Reagan	CONSERVATIVE

Is it any wonder that so many writers opposed President Reagan during the primaries and single-handedly kept the candidacy of John Anderson alive right down to the end—even though he espoused a radicalism that is totally out of step with Christianity, moral sanity, and free enterprise? It is a sad commentary on those who control our media, when five months before the election, less than 7 percent of our leading reporters and editors favored the man who ultimately became the overwhelming choice of the American people on election day. And don't be surprised when they criticize him: They didn't endorse him in the first place.

This media bias, which frequently demonstrates itself as anti free enterprise, should hardly come as a surprise; for in the 1972 presidential election between a moderate-liberal President Nixon and a superliberal Senator McGovern, in a similar straw vote, the same editors and reporters chose McGovern three to one, even though the American people later overwhelmingly rejected him at the polls. This and the 1980 elections verify what I have suspected for years: The press in this country is totally out of step with the people.

The principal reason we have so many elected officials who are out of step with the values of the American people is because the press is so out of step with us, and they have the power to promote their favorite candidates. The fact that a large majority of government leaders are not in accord with the populace at large was confirmed by a study involving 3,780 people; this study was made by Research and Forecasts Inc., who was commissioned by Connecticut Mutual Life Insurance in an attempt to "explore U.S. values of the 1980s and the extent to which they are shared by leaders."[1] Consider the following conclusions of this study:

> U.S. leaders are out of step with the public, which is more religious and more concerned about moral values than top people in most fields such as science, politics, the news media and education, a major study concludes.
>
> "It is clear there is a dramatic gap," John C. Pollock, the projects research director, said in a recent interview. "Overall, leaders are different from the public. They don't represent the public. . . ."
>
> Although there was no intent to focus on religion, it emerged as "the one factor that consistently and dramatically affects the values and behavior of Americans," the report said.
>
> "We had no idea we'd find this," Pollock said. "But there it was, showing up in every sort of systematic analysis, a common thread. It's more than a movement. It's something running through the whole culture."
>
> The 337-page report said the influence of religion "has penetrated virtually every dimension of American experience" and "is a stronger determinant of our values" than any other factor such as age, sex, economic status, race or whether a person is liberal or conservative.
>
> "Our findings suggest that the increasing impact of religion on our social and political institutions may be only the beginning of a trend that could change the face of America," it said.
>
> Moral issues have, "via religion, vaulted to the forefront of the

political dialogue . . ." the report said. "Something unusual is happening.

"American leaders are out of tune with the public which they are presumed to represent," the report added, saying the leaders are more flexible on moral issues and less religiously committed.[2]

You are probably wondering, *How could that be?* It is really very simple. Most major newspapers are owned by hard-core humanists or humanized thinkers. Only a handful of people own or control many of the newspapers in the country. The *Los Angeles Times,* which is owned by the Times Mirror Corporation, recently purchased the *Denver Post.* It already owned the *Times Herald,* in Dallas; *Connecticut Newspaper,* of Stamford, Connecticut; plus seven TV stations, three magazines, and four cable companies. *The New York Times* owns fourteen other American newspapers, two book publishing companies, five national magazines, and three TV stations. The Washington Post Company owns *Newsweek* magazine, the Daily Herald Publishing Company, the Trenton Times Corporation, and four TV stations. In addition, only two national wire services (Associated Press and United Press International) provide most newspapers with their daily news. Almost all the major editors of these papers (and hundreds like them) and the wire services' employees are committed humanists or humanized thinkers. That is, they consider religion unnecessary; morality optional, at best, or obsolete, at worst; and man perfectly capable of solving his own problems. They propose that the individual has a right to "do his own thing" and that a government-planned economy is preferable to free enterprise.

Let's not kid ourselves. The issue today is liberalism versus conservatism. Liberalism is based on humanistic thinking, conservatism on biblical principles. But our media are overwhelmingly controlled by liberal humanists, while the American people are predominantly conservative in both their views and their voting, whenever they can see through the media hype.

The media are also out of step with the American people because of the humanistic philosophy of most journalism schools. Only 35 percent of our young people go to college (surveys suggest that the more education a person has gained, the more likely he is to be liberal and to hold socialistic ideas. Some call that education; I call it brainwashing). The humanists discovered years ago that journalism schools were an excellent place to train the media editors and reporters of the future.

The Anti-Christian Bias of the Media

A classic illustration of the media bias occurred in April 1980. In response to a call for a day of prayer, 300,000 Christians marched on Washington, D.C. Except for the 1 million who appeared on the mall during the 1976 bicentennial celebration, that was the largest crowd in our nation's history. (The Christians even left the city cleaner than when they arrived, by carrying small plastic bags and picking up the debris.) One would think that such a record-breaking march on our nation's capital was news, but the papers didn't. To my knowledge, it was not carried on one front page in the country! In fact, many didn't even mention it, and those that did limited it to back-page trivia. Even TV blocked it out of the evening news.

Just three weeks later, fewer than 3,000 lesbians marched on Washington. The event hit the front page of every paper in the country and was carried on the evening TV news. Why? Our liberal humanist reporters and media controllers think more of 3,000 lesbians than they do of 300,000 Christians. Ironically, of course, this country was founded and made successful by Christians, not lesbians. But normalizing lesbianism by putting it on the front page is more within the interest span of our amoral humanist editors than advertising a public act of worship by Christians.

After watching this kind of news discrimination for half a century, I have come to expect it. But even I was not prepared for the media attacks on the Moral Majority that occurred during and after the 1980 elections. Was it really possible, I wondered, that peace-loving, morality-advocating ministers of the Gospel like Dr. Jerry Falwell could be compared to Adolph Hitler and Iran's Ayatollah Khomeini? If ever there was a distortion of the truth, it was the oft-repeated comparison of the "new religious right" with the Nazi party coming to power in Germany during the 30s. But to a hysterical humanist editor, terrified at the thought that his favored humanistic senators (who voted consistently for socialism and against free enterprise, who favored abortion and every other anti-moral stand of humanism) could not withstand conservative opposition, it seemed a fitting outburst.

A good illustration of their warped reporting appeared on the front page of a Los Angeles paper, three days after the election. Dr. Falwell was pictured together with the acknowledgment that the Moral Majority and other groups, such as the Religious Roundtable, Christian Voice, and Concerned Women for America, were largely responsible for the landslide victory that not only put Governor Ronald Reagan in the White House but swept ten conservative senators and thirty-three congressmen into office and retired an equal number of liberals. After making that reluctant confession, they proceeded to ask "religious leaders" what they thought of the emergence of the Moral Majority. Guess who they asked? Two liberal humanist ministers of the totally discredited National Council of Churches of Christ, a Unitarian minister, and a liberal Catholic priest. Why didn't they ask one of the pastors of the large, growing churches in California, any one of whom is influential to more people than all of those they interviewed put together? The predictable tactic of our biased press is to bring up a subject, then interview only those who agree with their humanist point of view. The media will dignify their opinions in the press and on TV as if they were the authorities, when in reality they are out of step with the people.

Every time I am invited to debate or participate on a TV program, the result is the same: The host and all the other guests appear in opposition to me or my position. Once when I participated in a sex-education panel discussion, I found the moderator and seven other panelists on one side, me on the other. So much for the fairness doctrine and objectivity!

The Power of TV News

TV has only been a news phenomenon in this country for thirty years. (In 1950 very few homes owned one; by 1980 there were more TVs in America than bathtubs.) It is estimated that almost 100 million people get most of their current events or news awareness from television. But is this medium "free" when less than 25 people, all of whom have strong humanistic leanings, on only three networks (CBS, ABC, and NBC), provide the interpretation of the news each night for 225 million people? No wonder that until the great voter revolt of 1980, TV's favorite politicians were elected and reelected to national offices.

The Vietnam era was probably the blackest and saddest period in American history. By its constant twisting of news stories to make America appear the aggressor, TV caused millions of our nation's youth to become disillusioned with their own country.

Dr. Ernest Lefever, director of Georgetown University Center for Ethics and Public Policy, has documented TV bias in a book and in public testimony, demonstrating that CBS provided "48 'dovish' views" (against American involvement) for every "one 'hawkish' (fight-to-win) view." For example, in a "CBS retrospective special on Vietnam, approximately three minutes was given to the deplorable My Lai incident in which U.S. soldiers killed 22 to 347 unarmed civilians, but the program failed to mention the cold-blooded murder of 2,700 to 5,000 civilians by the Communists in Hue during the 1968 Tet offensive. . . ."[3] Is it possible the media attack on Dr. Lefever that kept him out of the Reagan administration was in retaliation for this exposure of their duplicity?

Even today it is all but impossible to talk rationally to the average young person about Vietnam. Never does TV paint a picture of what life could have been for the current victims of the withdrawal of America's troops, after the media turned public opinion against the war. The crime in Vietnam was not our involvement but the death of 55,000 American boys who perished in a no-win war. If our military leaders had been given permission, in the early 70s, the war could easily have been won in one year. Millions of Vietnamese, Cambodians, and others would still be alive; and tragedies of the Boat People, refugees separated from their families, and starving children would have been avoided. But these results are rarely, if ever, mentioned. The media's opposition to a strong-America principle will not permit it. After two no-win wars (Korea and Vietnam), why did not the media cry out against asking our sons to risk their lives in a no-win war? They decry war on any basis—even for self-survival—but perceive no immorality in a no-win war. I pray God that America never again has to go to war, but if we do, it should be with a resolve to win as speedily as possible and with a minimum loss of life.

For years Walter Cronkite was the most watched newscaster in the country. Who can forget his deep, resonant voice as he recounted the newsworthy events each night? But like the others, he was opposed to a strong national defense.

> When Cronkite was asked by a Gannet News Service Reporter whether there was any substance to the charge in *TV and National Defense* that his evening show slighted "hawkish" views, he replied in the negative. But then he added three sentences . . . : "There are always groups in Washington expressing views of alarm over the state of our defenses. We don't carry those stories. The story is that there are those who want to cut defense spending."[4]

National newscasters prefer to interview those who agree with them and ignore those who represent the majority opinions of our people, thus serving as indoctrinators, rather than newscasters. We need a fairness doctrine that is fair to conservativism, which is the majority opinion. Better yet, we need one TV network that is committed to traditional conservative American values, the family, and patriotism. With such a medium, those of us who get tired of a constant parade of feminists, liberals, gay activists, kooks, and others selected by media humanists would have an alternative to shutting the TV off. Today, with the score three networks to zero, we have no other choice.

Another case in point occurred during the Republican National Convention in Detroit. During an interview, Senator Jesse Helms was called "a right-wing extremist." The North Carolina senator helped to hammer out a strong pro-moral, profamily, prolife and pro-American party platform that was later overwhelmingly approved by the American people. If Senator Jesse Helms, whom I have met personally as a Christian brother, is a "right-wing extremist," so are most of the American people.

To further demonstrate the media's so-called fairness, the same cameras focused upon former Senator Jacob Javits of New York, whom they described as "moderate." A look at Senator Javits' voting record will reveal that he concurred with Senators Kennedy, McGovern, and others on practically every liberal social program from abortion to welfare. If he is a moderate, there are no liberals! But that is the art in newscasting today. A handful of would-be opinion molders are masquerading as "newspersons," using their influence to gloss over the radicalism of their favored liberals, while heaping ridicule and scorn on those who represent the majority.

In *The Battle for the Mind,* I pointed out that all humanists are *not* Communists, but humanists and Communists are so similar that all Communists are humanists. That is why the humanist-controlled TV is often so favorable toward Communism and so derogatory (whenever they feel they can get away with it) toward America.

CBS and the Jim Jones Whitewash

In April 1980, CBS presented a TV documentary called "The Guyana Tragedy: The Story of Jim Jones," advertised as describing "the events that transformed the Rev. Jim Jones from the concerned leader of a movement for social justice to the charismatic personality who led the settlers of Jonestown, Guyana, into death."[5] No mention was made of the fact that Jim Jones was a socialist-Marxist-Communist.

John Loftin Jr., a reporter, gathering at least seven quotes from the *New York Times,* Washington *Post,* Chicago *Tribune* and other sources, all of which verified Jim Jones' Communist commitment, supplied them to the script writer before the show was aired. He was anxious to see if that important part of Jones's past would be mentioned. You guessed it: They refused his documented information! Loftin concluded:

> A CBS press release quoted Powers Boothe, the young actor who played Jim Jones, as saying: "I think that, somewhere along the line, Jones began to base his life on lies." Well, indeed he did. And the biggest of these lies was socialism, Marxism and communism. But you wouldn't have seen any of this on "Guyana Tragedy: The Story of Jim Jones."[6]

This kind of media distortion is neither rare nor accidental. Syndicated columnist Joseph Sobran has identified one means by which CBS deliberately uses semantics to promote its liberal humanist ideology:

> Why is it that the mass media so often seem to load their news coverage against the conservative side? I got a new clue to this abiding mystery the other day—and it came ironically in the form of an attempt to rid the news of bias.
>
> Anyone who works at CBS News (as I have done lately) is likely to receive a periodical guide to pronunciation and usage, compiled by Dr. Richard Norman. . . .
>
> On the abortion issue, he counsels newscasters and correspondents as follows:
>
> "In describing or referring to pro- or anti-abortion groups, the use of loaded terms should be avoided wherever possible. Many listeners might legitimately object to calling a pregnant woman a mother; calling a fetus or an embryo a child; and referring to an anti-abortion group as a 'pro-life' group or as 'right-to-life' advocates. . . ."[7]

As far back as we can trace the English language, pregnant women have regularly been considered "with child" or termed "expectant mothers." Why should CBS change it now? Because this shift in language takes the sting out of abortion. Killing a fetus or a mass or a living organism is not nearly as objectionable as killing a child. And calling antiabortionists prolife implies that abortionists are antilife, which is quite correct. Why doesn't CBS "tell it like it is"? Because they favor the liberal humanist philosophy that serves as the foundation of the pro-abortion lobby.

The Media Is Antifamily

By this time you may be thinking, *This is interesting, but what does it have to do with the battle for the family?* Quite frankly, the media are harmful to the family. For fifty years they have worked with their cohorts in education to condition the minds of voters to elect as many liberal humanists or liberal socialists as possible. Our stifling national debt, largely developed during the past thirty years, verifies the nature of their success. Their selection of the bizarre and perverted events of the day, presented as news, is just another attempt to subvert the "one man, one woman, so long as you both shall live" principle that undergirds the integrity of the family.

If you want an objective view of what is really happening today, you will probably have to look beyond your local paper, network news, and liberal magazines. Fortunately a slowly increasing number of conservative news sources furnishes an objective or conservative view of the world. One family I know experienced sharp conflict between the parents and their college-age son. The father and son constantly argued over political matters. Noting that only *Time, Newsweek,* the daily newspaper, and the nightly news influenced the young man, they could understand his liberalism. For Christmas they gave him magazine subscriptions to *U.S. News & World Report, Human Events,* and *Conservative Digest.* In less than one year he did a 75 percent turnaround in his philosophy. Naturally, his parents renewed the subscriptions.[8]

Media-Manipulated Elections

For over fifty years the media have been hyping, slanting, or distorting the news at election time, making it easy for the minority liberal humanists to be elected to office. In the primary, when voter interest is lowest and four or five candidates are running, the media select the most liberal Republican and the most liberal Democrat, then puff them, in the hope that in the general election the voters will have two liberals to choose from. If that doesn't work (though it has been successful in many areas of the country, popularizing the expression, "There isn't a nickel's worth of difference between the candidates"), they promote the liberal of their choice in the general election. This explains why America has been dominated by the minority (liberal humanist) view. The media so distorts the real issues that voters tend to elect candidates on the basis of party, looks, charisma, speaking ability, and popularity, without realizing what they really stand for.

The 1980 election was different because morality became the number-one burning issue in the hearts of millions of Americans. They went to the polls in enormous numbers to vote out of office those who had favored abortion, pornography, homosexuality, the ERA, and more government meddling in the family. These were moral issues that even the media couldn't disguise, although they tried. A flagrant distortion of the facts during the 1980 election is a case in point. Veteran senator Frank Church, with a vigorous liberal humanist voting record, was defeated by Idaho congressman Steve Symms. A committed conservative, Symms won by only 4,442 votes—or 1 percent. In a post-election interview, Senator Symms described the way in which the state's leading newspaper consistently used fictitious poll figures against him:

> The poll that got the most notoriety was done for the Boise paper owned by the Gannett conglomerate in New York. That paper was solidly favorable to Senator Church throughout the campaign, and regularly engaged in the wildest sort of personal attacks against me. It published a series of polls that started with Church as well ahead, then showed me 5.5 points behind, then said in two polls that we were tied. On the Sunday before the election it dropped its bomb with a headline story that claimed Church was leading me by nine percentage points. The paper said the data came from a poll of 800 households in the state.
>
> What made us suspicious was that the final poll claimed I was losing my own county—where I was raised and which I had always carried very strongly. I knew it was incorrect because our own polls showed I was well ahead there. But the national news media picked up that story and publicized it. On Monday, the day before the election, this story about "Church Leads Symms" was on the radio and television stations. That wasn't helpful.[9]

You may be wondering how Symms won over such media manipulation. Hard work and 18,000 volunteers, including many moral-majority Christians, who were concerned enough about their country to advertise the anti-moral voting record of the incumbent.

Until a sufficient number of wealthy Christian businessmen realize they should enter the media business, particularly TV and newspapers, as a means of saving our culture, we will continue to watch the liberal humanists who currently control them try to deceive the American voter into electing their favorite social liberals, who are more interested in controlling the family than in preserving it.

Another example of media misrepresentation relates to gun control. Every time there is a tragic attempt on some famous person's life, the media, particularly the TV newscasters, renew the call for gun control. When John Lennon was killed, and when President Reagan was shot, the press and TV immediately instituted lengthy discussions of gun control. I don't have space in this book for a discussion of its merits or demerits. I am simply reminding you that the media have been urging gun control for over thirty years, yet we still do not have it. Why? Because the overwhelming majority of the American people do not want it. Apparently no one in the media represents the vast majority. And as long as crime and violence stalk our streets, citizens will not willingly surrender their means of family protection.

If the media were influenced by true objectivity or fairness, why didn't some of them blame the movie *Taxidriver,* from which Hinkley, the president's would-be assassin, got his idea. That admission would lead to censorship. Better get guns away from the people, so they can no longer defend themselves.

Freedom of the press in America is an illusion! We only provide freedom for humanists to expound their liberal viewpoints. That fact came home to me this year when a reporter interviewed me for a profile. I sensed that I would receive a hatchet job, but it was worse than expected. My statements were so distorted and twisted that I still get letters from naive people, expressing their disappointment in me. That reporter has the "freedom" to judge me and present my life in as reprehensible a way as possible, in order to discredit me. Then her access to a major daily medium puts the report into the hands of thousands of people. I have the "freedom" to take it on the chin.

Why would a reporter who is supposed to be objective do something like that? Because she is a strong feminist. I am the California state president of the Moral Majority, and the word has gone out that local leaders of that movement should be "exposed." How do I know? Because as I travel, I find the same thing happening to leaders in Florida; Texas; Ohio; Illinois; Michigan; Washington, D.C.; and other places. "Freedom of the press" in reality is a freedom limited to the press, and our press is controlled by humanists.

Further evidence of the Los Angeles *Times* "objectivity" and adherence to "the fairness doctrine" was seen in the hatchet job they did on my friend Dr. Jerry Falwell. A reporter went to Lynchburg and took two days of Jerry's time, assuring him of a fair and honest treatment of a man whom I consider the most influential minister in America. After the article was published, they printed their diatribe in a twelve-page booklet, and the *Times* president sent complimentary copies to all 100 United States senators, 435 United States congressmen, and who knows who else. Why this attack on a minister of the Gospel? Like so many of our newspapers and TV telecasters, they are against voluntary prayers in school, traditional moral values, the church of Jesus Christ, a strong national defense, and many other things that Dr. Falwell favors.

As noted previously, what this country needs is a cooperative chain of newspapers committed to conservative thought and traditional moral values. Why shouldn't a city like Los Angeles have a liberal LA *Times* and a conservative alternate? The humanists were aware of the power of the press over one hundred years ago. They recognized that in order for a minority to control the majority, they had to control the press. Consequently when radio came along sixty years ago, they permeated its ranks, and they were ready to act just as quickly when TV appeared in the early 50s. Now that conservatives have awakened to the power of the media, will they be able to fashion a TV news network, wire service, and chain of newspapers? Only time will tell.

The Power of Media

To assert that the media (TV, newspapers, weekly magazines) through their presidential press conference have almost virtual control over our president may be an exaggeration. But to identify them as a dangerous, undemocratic engine that is working against the majority of our population is an understatement. When superliberal journalists and TV commentators could harrass the popular Lyndon Johnson right out of the White House, because he did something that displeased them, it is time to acknowledge the danger of their power.

Due to advances in radio, TV, and so on, press conferences have grown like Topsy in influence, until an elite group of self-appointed liberal critics can question our president in such a biased way that his views, motivations, and goals can be distorted and, in some cases, destroyed. One syndicated columnist admitted that because of them, ". . . I think we are in the era of one-term Presidents."

Richard Nixon was never one of my favorite politicians and did not claim my vote in 1968 or in 1972. In fact, I barely voted for him as governor of California in 1962. But as an American citizen I was grossly repulsed by the obnoxious, disrespectful way in which reporters quizzed him at his press conferences. Even President Carter was humiliated by their arrogant manners on some occasions.

One reporter defends the nationally televised conferences (which I call presidential grillings) as necessary to "let the President know what the public is thinking." That is nonsense! Such biased questioning only forces the public to learn what the liberal press wants it to know, for they are the only ones present. And this is often contrary to the best interests of a nation that was based on traditional Judeo-Christian moral values and the free-enterprise system. To make such conferences meaningful, we should either let our presidents give reports to the American people, uncluttered by biased comments, so each citizen can make up his own mind, or have equal representation—a conservative question for every liberal question. With such a procedure, both sides could be aired. That certainly is not the case now on our public airways.

One of the features in Orwell's *1984* was "Newspeak." Each evening Big Brother invaded the home via the TV set to speak to the citizens and interpret the day's news in the light of the official government line. We laughed back in 1952, considering that preposterous. Today, because of our national fascination with TV news, more people receive their news interpreted by liberal commentators than by any other means. And our media, subject to minimal governmental control, are regulated stringently by a handful of liberal people.

Americans pride themselves on their free press or free media. But how free is it in a pluralistic society, when one side controls all the media? Name, for example, one network or newscaster representing the conservative point of view. You cannot name one! Yet in 1980 conservatives elected a conservative president, ten conservative senators, and thirty-three new conservative congressmen, by a landslide. Shouldn't that majority be represented by the media?

Consider, for example, the subject of censorship. If a discussion involves ridding the schools, public libraries, or newsstands of pornographic or other morally degrading literature, all three networks invariably introduce the subject of censorship and First Amendment violations. Not one newscaster will think to ask, "How do pornographic books, paid for with taxpayer's money, get into those libraries in the first place? Who is making the decision to put mind-polluting literature within easy reach of innocent children? Does the First Amendment guarantee that merely because it is in print, any morally degrading book, written by a morally sick mind, should be placed in public libraries with public monies?" A conservative newscaster would ask such questions. But our newscasters have a knee-jerk reaction to any suggestion that we upgrade the moral quality of our libraries by elimination of filthy material, responding as if we were Adolph Hitler on a vigilante crusade to exterminate the Jews.

It is the same on every issue. I chuckled at Mike Wallace's change of attitude while interviewing Mel and Norma Gabler, the famous textbook evaluators, in Dallas. During a "Sixty Minutes" interview with Mrs. Gabler, he showed his usual bias toward anyone who criticizes the indecency in our textbooks. Mrs. Gabler spontaneously asked him to read something prepared for sixth graders. Suddenly he stopped in the middle of a sentence. He had come to a word so filthy that it was illegal to use it on national TV. To his credit, he changed his attitude during the rest of the interview, evidently convinced that sex education was no longer the wholesome health education with which he was familiar.

What America needs is a fourth TV network, a newspaper wire service, and a chain of conservative newspapers to offer an alternative to the liberal humanist fare now offered on our existing outlets. Such an optional source of news and entertainment would probably bankrupt the liberal networks, for people watch them today primarily because no alternative exists. When you pray for your country, ask God to give us a wholesome media alternative. That would be true "pluralism." But don't expect our humanist friends to respond favorably to that suggestion. They have known for years what we are just waking up to: The minority can only control the majority when they control the media.

Freedom of the press only works when you also have responsibility in journalism. Today there is no one to guarantee such responsibility. That is why we need local, state,and national review boards to command the objectivity and competence of journalists or to publicly rebuke them when they have abused the power of the press. As it is, no such review board exists, and each managing editor acts as his own judge and jury of fairness. If the FCC needs a fairness doctrine and if the police need review boards, why not a fairness in media review board for the press and TV?

Notes

1. "Leaders Found Short on Religion," *Union* (South Dakota) (3 April 1981), p. A–12.
2. *Ibid.*
3. Ernest W. Lefever, "CBS: The News Twisters," *Conservative Digest* 6 (April 1980), p. 23.
4. *Ibid.*
5. John D. Loftin, Jr., "Why Did CBS Ignore Jim Jones' Communist Leanings?" *Human Events* 40 (3 May 1980), p. 18.
6. *Ibid.*
7. Joseph Sobran, "Are Babies Taboo?" *World* (Tulsa) (3 July 1980, p. 12A).
8. If you would like an address list of family-oriented and conservative magazines and newspapers, just send a self-addressed, stamped envelope to Family Life Seminars, P.O. Box 1299, El Cajon, CA 92022.
9. John Rees, "Senator-Elect Steve Symms," *The Review of the News* 16 (26 November 1980), pp. 43, 44.

Feminism

One of the ironies of history is that the feminist movement is strongest in the country that provides the world's finest conditions for women. That is not to say that women are not discriminated

against in America. Women should receive equal pay for equal work, and a qualified woman should be given just as much consideration and advancement as an equally qualified man. Sad to say, that is not always the case.

The rapid rise of the feminist movement is ample proof that inequities in our society need to be addressed. Many of these discriminatory practices have been rectified, but some have not. One of my pet peeves is the unbiblical practice of giving men more social-security pay than their wives. While a case can be made for the wife of a retired man receiving less, since two living together is a little cheaper than two living separately, when he dies, his widow should receive the full amount. The fact that he worked out of the home and paid social-security taxes has nothing to do with it. If he paid, she paid! In the Bible, the soldiers who "stayed with the stuff" behind the lines received the same share in the spoils of war as those who fought in the battle.

While a feminist movement has been visible ever since the 1800s, in the last twenty years it has come into special prominence. Betty Friedan, sometimes called the mother of the feminist movement, articulated the values and dreams of feminism in the early 60s and went on to found NOW (National Organization of Women). With its 100,000 members (according to NOW, though outsiders are not permitted to verify that membership figure), NOW is usually identified as the most powerful of the feminist organizations. Originally, they campaigned on a platform of liberating women from male chauvinism and despotism. Demanding equal rights, equal job opportunities, the right to control their own bodies, and ultimately the right to choose their own sexual orientation, they have made enormous inroads in our society. "Sexist language" has been eliminated from our children's school texts and government publications. Chairmen of organizations and meetings have been transformed into *chairpersons.* Even God has not escaped their wrath, for the liberal National Council of Churches of Christ has just endorsed a radical new Bible that addresses "Our Parent who art in Heaven" instead of "Our Father." Since most hard-core feminists don't believe in the God of the Bible, why not address Him as *her?*

In the early days of the feminist movement, most men ignored it, flinching at some of its extreme emphases, but hopeful that it would correct some of the obvious inequities in our society. Gradually, however, it fell into the hands of angry radicals who have all but ruined the movement.

ERA: Feminist Cornerstone

The Equal Rights Amendment is a good illustration of the movement itself. Ratified quickly by the Senate and House of Representatives, in 1972, it was railroaded through thirty-four states before serious questions surfaced. Would the Equal Rights Amendment legalize homosexuality, making it possible for homosexual schoolteachers to flaunt their position as an optional life-style, in our public schools? Would it make it impossible to refuse to hire a known homosexual or force employers, through affirmative action and job quotas, to fire heterosexuals and hire homosexuals? Would landlords have to rent to known homosexuals? Would the courts have to record homosexual marriages and give known homosexuals child custody? Would girls be eligible for the draft against their will, and would women be forced into combat? Many lawyers responded with a resounding *yes!* including former senator Sam Ervin (Democrat from North Carolina), known and respected on both sides of the aisle as a constitutional authority. Concurring statements appeared in the prestigious *Yale Law Journal* and *Harvard Law Journal*.

Phyllis Schlafly, the wife of a prominent Illinois lawyer and mother of six, who finished law school while raising her family, began to perceive the dangers of this movement and organized Eagle Forum and Stop ERA. Single-handedly she has awakened an army of followers, and scores of other organizations have joined her fight, until now it appears that they have successfully killed the ERA, in spite of its illegal three-and-one-half-year extension period. Mrs. Schlafly should go down in history as having done more for the present and future families and children of America than any other person in the 1970s.

ERA Is Superfluous

All feminists campaign for the Equal Rights Amendment on a platform that guarantees equal pay for equal work and equal job opportunities. In my wife's new book she clarifies, "There is already legislation in operation that deals with such forms of discrimination between the sexes."[1] As proof, she cites the following:

Equal pay for equal work is covered by:
    Civil Rights Act of 1964
    Equal Pay Act of 1963
    Equal Employment Opportunity Act of 1972
Equal treatment is covered by:
    Fourteenth Amendment
    Higher Education Act of 1972
    Comprehensive Health Manpower Training Act of 1971
    Nurse Training Act of 1971
    Comprehensive Employment and Training Act of 1973
    Federal Equal Credit Opportunity Act of 1975[2]

She continues:

Because of these existing laws, millions of dollars have been received by women whose cases against large corporations in our country were brought to court. Some complain that even though we have these laws, there are still inequities and discrimination. If the laws are not being properly enforced, the solution is to strengthen and expand the services that implement the laws already in existence, not create new laws that make enforcement an even greater problem.

The passage of the ERA would not eliminate economic and social injustices. The legal process we now have would still be necessary, to correct illegal actions.[3]

In late 1980 the courts demonstrated just how effective those laws are. In response to a suit by some female employees, the Ford Motor Company was ordered by the courts to pay $23 million in back wages for unequal pay. The feminists never tell their followers that even if ERA passed tomorrow, individual women would still have to take discriminatory practices to the courts, to have justice done. If they must go to court anyhow, and if effective laws to help women are already on the books, who needs the ERA? Not women as a sex but lesbians and homosexuals need the ERA; and believe me, that's what it's really all about! Homosexuals and lesbians, who number perhaps 6 percent of the population, recognize their unpopular status. They decided early that the feminist movement and the ERA provided them with a handy vehicle to ride piggyback upon "women's rights" and achieve homosexual rights. Fortunately, citizens who suddenly realized how close we were to the city limits of Sodom and Gomorrah successfully resisted the ERA.

Who Favors the ERA, Anyway?

Although we can't always tell a book by its cover, we can usually determine the moral worth of something by examining its principal supporters. In recent years the smoglike confusion feminists have spread over the subject has confused many women and men about ERA. Consequently, even some contented housewives can be numbered among its supporters. But I have detected that most of its loudest defenders are hostile, overbearing, vocal humanists like Bella Abzug, Humanist of the Year award winner (1975), Betty Friedan (who also signed *Humanist Manifesto II*), and Gloria Steinem (who delivered such a vile anti-Christian diatribe in a speech at Pepperdine University that I wouldn't even reprint it). Other leading lights of the feminist movement are acknowledged lesbians, which probably accounts for the despicable homosexual displays at the IYC convention in Houston and the annual NOW convention in Los Angeles, in 1980 (to which we sent a representative to gain firsthand information and from whom we learned that dildos, vibrators, and other lesbian paraphernalia that would shock any decent person were openly displayed).

Have you reviewed the list of the organizations that were among the original promoters of the Equal Rights Amendment? Consider the following, by no means a complete list:

National Organization of Women
National Gay Task Force
American Humanist Association

American Ethical Union
Unitarian Universalist Association
National Council of Churches of Christ
Socialist Feminist Commission
Communist Party, U.S.A.
American Civil Liberties Union
United Nations Commission on Women

These are only some of the radical organizations that actively promote ERA. At this juncture we must ask, "If the ERA supported the good of America, the family, and specifically women, why would these organizations promote it?" It is the one piece of legislation that would do more to destroy the traditional family in this country than any other they have advocated. That is why it is so difficult for them to realize that it has been rejected by the overwhelming majority of the morally minded American people.

Feminism's Effects on the Family

The harmful gains of the feminist movement between 1976 and 1980 will do injury to America for many years to come. I hope the new trends back toward traditional moral values will undo some of these policies. Presently, however, we are reaping a number of results that I view as threats to the family, unless the feminist movement is exposed for what it truly is: a group of radicals who claim to speak for the American woman but in truth misrepresent her and use womanhood to advance the cause of homosexuality, lesbianism, and radicalism. Consider some of these harmful effects on the family:

1. Creates Unnecessary Competition Between Husband and Wife Married partners should be lovers, not competitors. But the drive to take women out of the kitchen and compel them to compete on an equal basis with men is not conducive to the promotion of harmony between mates. A true partnership is based on interdependency: two people who are complementary to each other. Just as one cannot unilaterally procreate another human being, but must sexually complement a mate in that function, so in many other areas the husband and wife function best together. In fact, the best marriages are those in which the partners appreciate each other's distinctive gifts and realize they can accomplish far more by co-operation with each other than either could achieve alone. This awareness will inspire the willingness to sacrifice their individual self-centered desires for the greater corporate good. Couples need each other and will never be truly happy until they realize that. The feminist obsession with "my rights as a woman" often comes at the expense of a woman's rights and responsibilities as a wife. This usually leads to hostility in a marriage.

2. *Blurs the Distinction Between the Sexes* The unisex emphasis in education is the result of feminist intimidation of the state and federal school system. Actually, it is a debasement of women, tantamount to suggesting that being a woman is somehow a second-rate position. Rather than featuring her femininity, she is treated as a unisex object.

The refusal to face the differences between men and women borders on intellectual insanity. Ordinary people have no difficulty admitting these differences, none of which denotes inferiority, but all of which signal exciting diversity.

Consider some of these:

1. Sexuality—physiologically the sexes obviously differ.
2. Maternal instinct—women, not men, instinctively yearn to nurture, love, and care for the young.
3. Physical capacity—all the feminist rhetoric in the world will not alter the fact that men have stronger upper bodies than women and can usually run and swim faster.
4. Aggressiveness—men pick more quarrels, seem more combative, are sexually the perpetrators of rape, and so on.
5. Emotional vacillation—women experience greater mood alterations. It is a fact of nature that men never have periods and never give birth to children. One scientific writer claims that women have from two to six times as much difficulty with depression as men.[4]

The Bible teaches us that, in the beginning, God made them male and female. If He had wanted only men, He could have arranged it that way. But instead He designed us sexually different and endorsed procreation in marriage, while condemning all forms of same-sex activity. The feminist movement is in part a fight against God and nature, which is one reason it is doomed to failure. Fortunately, it has not been able to convince the majority of American women.

3. Creates Unnecessary Dissatisfaction With Being a Housewife and Mother Feminist educators have succeeded in changing even the pictures of women in our children's textbooks. An order out of Sacramento forbids the inclusion of pictures in our school texts depicting women with aprons and vacuums. Men are now shown doing housework, and women are depicted as mechanics, telephone repairpersons, and so on. Such distorted concepts make little girls unnecessarily career oriented and cause housewives to become dissatisfied with their role and bored with homelife. Many develop a risky obsession with going to work, which in turn may become tiring and boring. Some have needlessly sacrificed their marriage in a quest to follow the feminist illusion.

4. Causes Insecurity in Women It is imperative that everyone come to grips with himself: who he is and why he is here. Many women today are being driven by the feminist mentality to assume an aggressive posture that is not conducive to self-acceptance and a feeling of emotional security.

After studying many disturbed women, Maggie Scarf makes this frightening admission:

> ... women are vulnerable to depression because emotional attachments are much more important to them than to men. In many cases, she says, women define themselves almost exclusively by their relationships to others. When these bonds break—through death, divorce or children leaving home—they often suffer depression. Some say they would rather kill themselves than live alone. . . .
>
> These apparent differences raise a troubling possibility: that emotional bonding, once a key to survival, is making women's lives more difficult in today's feminist era. Women are caught between

the demands of their genes, urging them toward marriage and family, and a society sending them powerful new signals to be independent. While Scarf admits that men also suffer from depression, she says that the condition is usually triggered by failure in their profession, not in their personal relationships. It might seem logical that women who follow men into the marketplace would be less vulnerable to depression. Not so, says Scarf. The working women she studied were just as depressed as those who stayed at home, reinforcing her unsettling conviction that mood is a function of biology.[5]

Phyllis Chesler, a psychologist and a hard-line feminist, author of three best-selling books in favor of the feminist movement, woke up just in time. At thirty-seven she recognized that she would soon lose the physical capacity to be a mother, so she made what she described as " 'the most courageous decision of my life'—to have a baby." Although traditional moralists do not approve of her decision to have a child out of wedlock, her experience with her feminist friends is nevertheless interesting. "It was a very isolated, frightening time for me," Ms. Chesler said in an interview. "My friends thought I had gone mad, that somehow I had deserted the cause. But I had reached a point where it became clear to me that my work, art, writing was not enough. The unique intimacy and transcendence offered in the birth of a child was something I didn't want to deny myself."

When her son Ariel was born two years ago, Ms. Chesler admitted, "I felt like an impostor. 'Do I look like a mother?' I wondered. 'What's a feminist doing as a mother?' I thought."

For a year she stopped visiting her feminist friends in New York City where she lives and they stopped coming over.

"I was demoted. They had warned me it would be the end of my career, that I'd regret it, that I'd become isolated," she recalled.

"Ironically, I don't think I could have become a mother if I didn't learn courage from feminism. I was filled with fear about such things as what I would do when I was alone with the baby."

Snubbed by her former colleagues, she began to seek companionship with other new mothers.

"Sitting on park benches with them, I realized how afraid women are of speaking to each other. One young mother told me, 'After I gave birth, I could only talk to other mothers. But I was afraid to tell them the real truth. So I couldn't trust what they said either. . . .' "

"The birth of my baby transformed me forever. . . ."[6]

There is something fulfilling about motherhood that cannot be matched on any other level.

5. Destroys Femininity   I have attended enough feminist rallies and debates with my wife, Bev (who, as president of Concerned Women for America, is often forced to oppose their programs and ideology), to know that many feminists look and act more like blocking ends in the NFL than women. In fact, one of the characteristics that defeated the ERA was the unfeminine conduct and image of many of the feminist leaders.

Let's face it, there is nothing feminine about sloppy jeans and T-shirts. Many career women of courage dress stylishly, but even some of them project the idea that they wish they were men. What's wrong with femininity? There is something ennobling and enriching in a woman dressing and acting as if she is proud to be a woman.

I was pleased with a comment by a national magazine reporter after she interviewed Bev at length. Writing a book to be titled *The Death of the ERA,* that reporter volunteered, "I have really been impressed with your wife; she is so feminine. My research has brought me into contact with most of the leaders of the feminist movement, but as a woman, I seem to relate to Beverly better than any of them." And this came from a woman who considered herself a feminist.

Femininity by no means indicates weaknesses. It does, however, denote womanliness, strength, virtue, modesty, and grace. Our nation's girls need to start thinking of themselves as ladies with a purpose in life to fulfill, instead of as animals with appetites to be satisfied, as so many feminist humanists envision them.

6. Causes Insecurity in Men   A good man usually brings out the best instincts in a woman, just as a good woman enables a man to make the most of his masculinity. God intended man to be the provider, protector, leader, and priest for his wife and family. Feminism tends to destroy that. Instead of allowing the man to assume and become comfortable in his appointed role, the feminist movement tends to destroy man's natural identity and force him to compete with the very person he should cooperate with and protect.

Feminism is the ultimate in selfishness. It appeals to "my rights," "my goals," "my feelings"; consequently it destroys whatever it touches. Historically and biblically, selfishness has always been a destroyer. God challenges us, "Give and it shall be given unto you." Feminism is not interested in giving—it takes.

Unfortunately, feminism forces women to be the greatest losers. The woman whose unfeminine feminism drives men away in her youth by making them feel insecure around her is doomed to spend her life in lonely solitude. Most men don't fight against the feminist movement, and few will speak out against it. They prefer to ignore it. With a population of 9 percent more women than men, feminists are largely disregarded. As a result, I predict that in the years to come there will be a tragic increase in depression and suicide among the forty- to fifty-year-old former feminists.

If you sense that feminists are against men *and* women (feminine women at least), you are right on target. Actually I get suspicious that they are more interested in overthrowing our traditional social order than in securing "human rights" or "women's rights."

7. *Makes Children Insecure* Most credible child authorities are registering alarm at the enormous increase in insecurity among children. The feminist's obsession with creating a unisex or antifeminine society makes children insecure about themselves, their sexual identities, and their sex direction. When a parent feels comfortable in his own gender, the child will accept his. Conversely the parent who rejects his sex can predispose his child to reject his.

A heartbroken mother in the East told the story of her twenty-year-old daughter, who came home from a liberal denominational church college to confess, "I'm gay." She had roomed with a lesbian who had taught her that life-style. Under questioning the mother revealed that she had always wanted to be a boy, so she related well to her three sons. Apparently she had been so distressed when her fourth pregnancy resulted in a baby girl that without realizing it, she had communicated her disappointment to the child, who tried to act like a boy all through school. Consequently, though an honor student through high school, she had no time for boys or dates. In actuality, since early childhood, she had not liked being a girl because her mother didn't seem to accept her womanhood.

Admittedly, all feminists don't reject their feminine characteristics. However, many give that impression, and if girls detect that in the home, they will conclude that being a woman is second-rate.

Notes

1. Beverly LaHaye, *I Am a Woman by God's Design* (Old Tappan, N.J.: Revell, 1980), p. 132.
2. Eileen Vogel, *Abortion and the Equal Rights Amendment: A Call to Common Sense* (Pittsburgh: People Concerned for the Unborn Child, 1978), pp. 2, 3.
3. LaHaye, pp. 132, 133.
4. Cynthia H. Wilson and Eric Gelman, "Why Women Are Depressed," *Newsweek* 94 (8 September 1980), p. 81.
5. *Ibid.*
6. "Noted Feminist in New Role: Being a Mother," Lowell *Sun* (9 May 1980).

8

Materialism

"But seek first the kingdom of God and His righteousness, and all these things will be added to you."

Matthew 6:33 NKJV–NT

"My husband wants me to go to work full-time, yet we still have a five-month-old baby at home. To be a submissive wife, must I get a job?" asked a young wife during the question period at one of our

Family Life Seminars. Upon further inquiry we discovered that the "necessity" for the wife to go to work involved neither unpaid bills nor money to pay the rent. Instead, electric power tools had become essential on her young husband's materialistic list.

Before you laugh, ask yourself sometime, "Is this trip, purchase, or want really necessary?" Everyone is vulnerable to the temptations of materialism in some form. That's why the Bible admonishes, "Love not the world, neither the things that are in the world. If any man love the world, the love of the Father is not in him" (1 John 2:15). Your problem area may be food, cars, clothes, or a hundred other items, but be sure of this: You are vulnerable to some enticing area of materialism. That is why TV advertisers will pay up to $275,000 per minute for prime-time commercials.

Financial Problems and Divorce

Almost every family counselor I know admits that financial difficulties are one of the leading causes of divorce, particularly among the young. That is understandable, both from the standpoint of their youthful inexperience and the incredibly high cost of living. Most young couples are hopelessly in debt shortly after marriage.

It is natural for young couples to aspire to the living standard of their parents as they set up post-honeymoon housekeeping. The fact that it took their folks twenty or thirty years of work, saving, and sacrifice in order to reach their present level doesn't usually occur to young lovers. Consequently they charge the furniture they cannot afford, pay excessive rent, and drive a car upon which they owe more than it is worth. No longer are vehicles merely a means of transportation; they have become a peer-pressure status symbol. And the passage of years authorizes a parade of fads, from pickups, vans, jeeps, and four-wheelers, to the latest "in" thing.

Before marriage, life is quite simple, for dating costs are relatively light. But since living at home cannot compare to setting up housekeeping, young married people are ill-prepared for marriage and the hidden costs of married life.

If it appears that I am discouraging young people from getting married, you're wrong. However, I want them to see that plunging into the financial bondage of credit buying puts an unnatural strain on any family, particularly young people in the adjustment stage.

Interest rates that have soared to 23 percent in some places can mean that we will pay twice the value of a purchase if we buy on credit. Our government is certainly no fiscal model in this regard, for we are rapidly approaching a national debt of $1 trillion. The interest alone on that debt is over $100 billion annually, equivalent to the total appropriations by our federal government in 1963. Symptomatic of our age, the majority of our nation, following the example of government, heeds the call of the money lenders to "buy now, pay later."

Here is a good rule of thumb for any couple: Buy nothing on credit except a house or car, and even these should always be worth more than is owed upon them. In addition, no more than 35 percent of one's income should go to these payments. All other purchases should be paid in cash that has been saved up. You will be amazed at how many material objects you can do without while waiting to save your money to buy something.

To most families, credit is a financial way of life. Currently there seems to be a contest between the bankers and our nation's families as to how much interest people will tolerate before rejecting the buy-on-time philosophy. For years they were satisfied with 8 percent or 10 percent. My banker reminded me recently that I refused a 12 percent construction loan because I considered the figure temporarily high. Cautioning that bankers in America have watched their counterparts in Europe charge as much as 26 percent, he expressed the belief that high interest rates were a permanent feature of the American scene. These high interest rates and credit buying make it almost impossible for young couples to purchase a home without help from their parents.

The Credit-Card Curse

The financial bondage of families is often caused by the curse of credit cards, which make it easy to borrow against the future instead of saving for it. Countless family arguments are ignited when one member (usually the one with the least sales resistance) cannot forego the temptation to use his or her plastic magic-kingdom card. Judgment day comes at the end of the month, causing sparks that often create a needless fire.

How well do I remember, when our children were small (matching my salary) that we took an extended speaking trip by way of those attractive credit cards. The trip cost much more than we expected, so I used the expense checks I received for travel reimbursement. When my credit-card statement came a month later, it was literally out of sight. In fact, it totaled one month's salary. We immediately made the decision to destroy all credit cards. I wrote letters to the companies, confessing what I had done and begging their patience, then spent the next eighteen months whittling that debt down to size. From that day to this I have paid cash for all gasoline purchased for personal use. Now I recommend that credit cards be limited to business expenses only, when for tax purposes it is an asset for accounting. Otherwise, the pay-as-you-go method forces an individual to spend only for what is essential. But even more important, it helps young couples avoid those unnecessary marital pressure spots that engender strife.

House Size Versus Quality

The size of a house never indicates the quality of love found within. Our Lord said, "A man's life does not consist of those things which he possesses." Americans need to learn that lesson! Obsessed as we are with the "good life," people of all ages seem bent on seeking first their place in the sun, instead of in the kingdom of God. I have yet to find a person who was dominated by a quest for riches, who enjoyed contentment. Yet the Lord said, "Godliness with contentment is great gain" (1 Timothy 6:6).

Recently I shared with our congregation the counseling I had given that weekend to a couple having difficulty communicating because they were nonstop TV watchers. Afterwards a wife remarked, "Our TV just broke. Your story has inspired me to leave it that way." Three months later she added, "Not having TV has been a blessing to our whole family; we now talk freely and have learned to play games together." Within six months she was in the hospital with cancer, and three months later she went to be with the Lord. Some of the family's happiest moments were partially the result of materialistic deficiency: the absence of funds to repair the TV. As a consequence, one family designed a fabric of unity and harmony that riches could not weave.

A false standard of living, a higher anxiety level, and family squabbles are a natural result of submission to the god of things. The family that seeks the kingdom of God long before it worships at the altar of materialism will inherit untold blessings and avoid the Slough of Impoverishment, which invariably engulfs those whose affections are set on wordly possessions.

One family in our church experienced severe financial difficulty for a period of two years. They didn't get behind on the mortgage or forego regular meals, but special treats, such as eating out or attending the symphony, were suspended for the duration, and the budget could not handle most activity requests from the family teenagers. Thus when Johnny would plead, "But dad, my Sunday-school class is going to Disneyland on Saturday, and I need ten dollars," dad would respond, "Just how do you plan to raise the ten dollars?" Instead of creating dissension and strife, the absence of "funds for fun" caused Johnny to rethink his priorities, program strategies for financing special occasions, and develop fiscal self-reliance. Materialistic hardships bred three family benefits:

1. Children who learned the value of the dollar
2. A new family awareness of "needs"
3. Increased dependence upon God's provision

Almost miraculously the youngsters found new baby-sitting or lawn jobs that supplied each urgent request. As one teenager commented after the long ordeal was over, "God has promised to supply our needs, and He does a remarkable job of funding our druthers."

Materialism can be a serious threat to the family—if you let it.

9

Urbanization: A Subtle Threat to the Family

Home is one of the most beautiful words in any language. In a vicious, competitive, and often dangerous world, *home*, even when

it describes a humble thatch hut with a dirt floor, has come to be universally regarded as a haven to which all family members can retreat in order to recharge their emotional and spiritual batteries. With this strength they can once again face the hostile world.

"Be it ever so humble, there is no place like home." Not a syrupy or meaningless maxim, it describes the heart yearning, I would suspect, of more than 99 percent of all the people who have ever lived—regardless of their race, language, or culture. Occasionally we find someone whose home was so hellish that it was impossible to bear, but even then an individual seeks for a substitute home of some sort.

Ever since the Industrial Revolution, home has been changing—not only in size and shape, but in location. At one time most people seldom traveled more than 200 miles from the place they were born. Consequently they knew all their neighbors for miles around. In fact, it was not uncommon in many villages and towns for an individual to be related to 20 percent of the area's population.

An interesting comparison between past and present appeared in Alvin Toffler's *Future Shock:*

> In 1914 the average American totalled perhaps 1,600 miles of travel per year. By 1970 the American car owner alone travelled over 10,000 miles each year, and during his lifetime an individual would cover approximately three million miles—more than thirty times the total lifetime travel of the 1914 American. Highway mileage increased 100% during a time when our population rose only 38.5%.[1]

Since those figures were compiled, travel has multiplied at an incredible rate. During that time we have gone from jets to jumbo jets and are now being introduced to super jumbos. The same transience can be found in Europe and even some of the backward countries of the world, which are starting to emerge.

The Flight to the City

All over the world the migration to the city has produced unbelievable traffic jams, noise pollution, air contamination, and most harmful of all, family deterioration. In an attempt to capture a part of the "good life" (a job, a home, a car, an education for the children, TV, and "some of the comforts of life"), millions of people have sacrificed the most priceless asset in life: the family. It reminds one of the man in South Africa who sold his small farm to "strike it rich" in the city, only to find that the new owners discovered acres of diamonds on his old farm property.

The millions who left the safety and love of the village for the new job in the city never dreamed that the road to progress was paved with the heartaches of millions who had previously encountered much higher rates of greed, selfishness, immorality, crowded working conditions, loss of freedom, impersonalization, and in many cases, the loss of those dearest to them. Some people can make the transition to an impersonal way of life. Those who do, however, may find it difficult to cope in an environment that is conducive to a myriad of human contacts limited to, "Hi," "Good morning," "How are you?" or even "Have a nice day." They will probably surmise that whether they live or die, no one in the neighborhood, apartment, or housing project will notice, and even then they may not care.

As Toffler points out, much of the existential rhetoric that millions of young people read censures "modular man" (fragmented relationships) and encourages "total involvement."[2] Personally, I would suspect they are crying for the constancy of an intimate love relationship with a small number of people. Everyone craves what can only be found in the family. Brief and transitory brushes with other human beings cannot form a substitute.

Having ministered in California for twenty-five years, I have watched many who left the security of home and came to our "land of opportunity," then scurried back to their more stable homes and unfulfilled dreams, tarnished by divorce, teenage pregnancy, or just a yearning for the intimacy with family members they once took for granted. And these are predominantly church-oriented people. It must be far more frightening to those who do not find a haven in a Bible-teaching church.

Urbania Is Not Utopia

Everything is intensified in the city: crime, violence, sex, drugs, divorce, insecurity, and people. We were all shocked a few years ago when a woman in New York City was beaten to death in broad daylight, with thirty-nine people watching from apartment windows, cars, and street corners—and no one went to her aid. Finally an old woman fearfully called the police. That isn't living: It is an animal existence.

By any set of statistics, life in the big city is more oppressive than town people may be led to believe. Divorce rates skyrocket with the size of the city. It is claimed that 50 percent of all teenage pregnancies occur in the ghettos. The inner city has a much higher VD rate, and in the same area crime is rampant. Welfare, rarely the true friend of the poor, has resulted in drawing the poor into a concentrated inner-city area where the viciously strong take advantage of the weak. Human suffering in such areas is beyond the imagination of those who do not live there. We are experiencing a return to nature, out into the woods, fields, and mountains; but for millions the city is an economic necessity that will haunt us long into the twenty-first century.

Is Suburbia Better?

Since World War II the move to suburbia has only served to enlarge our urban problems. True, they are not as intensified as those of the inner city, but they are real and very similar. A new book, purportedly based on seven years of research, portrays the morals of suburbia as little better than sexually active high-school classes. If the author's suggestions are only half true, promiscuity in the suburbs has made a mockery of marital fidelity.

Crime and vandalism are as bad in the suburban community as in the ghetto, if allowance is made for a lower concentration of people. Just a few miles from my home, in one of our nicer suburbs, on Christmas day neighbors noticed no movement whatever in a fashionable home. Upon investigation they discovered four bodies. In despair at the prospect of losing his home to divorce, the father had shot his wife, two children, and then himself. Suburban living certainly failed them.

It is not uncommon today for suburbanites not to know their neighbors by name or sight. Some are so preoccupied with their own cares that they become indifferent to the needs of others. We live in a day of impersonality.

When most Americans did not travel very far in their lifetimes, it was fashionable to "be your brother's keeper." When people went to town, they knew many of the other townsfolk, and that had a stabilizing influence on many families. At times of infatuation with someone other than one's mate, social pressures caused many to resist making a hasty decision until the alienation-of-affection feeling passed, thwarting unnecessary divorces. Weighed in the light of the millions of fatherless children or single-parent families, today's lifestyle may be termed more progressive, but I question if it's better.

The Extended Family

When our family came to California, twenty-five years ago, only one out of eight people was born here; consequently we saw few extended families. One would suspect that it was easier to raise children when they were surrounded by relatives. A teenager could hardly do wrong in the "old days" without his parents finding out. If he was kicked out of school, half the people he passed on the road home were aunts, uncles, and cousins. His mother had probably received half a dozen reports before he walked in the front door.

Not only was that helpful in cutting down the teenage yen for rebellion, but it had a marked influence on self-image and gave a sense of security. Every child belonged to someone—in fact, lots of people. Today's impersonalized life-style does nothing to engender the notion that every individual is important to someone and is loved by others.

Through the years our church has proved to be a magnetic attraction to both Bev's and my relatives so that almost all have moved out here, and our children have grown up and married in the church. Consequently our family gatherings are reminiscent of the "good old days." Last Christmas I saw a beautiful example. My grandsons Joel and Joshua had to go to bed before the party was over, so they made a big production of jumping from one lap to another—including grandparents, uncles, aunts, cousins, and parents—in order to get a good-night kiss. While watching this, I realized that God intended such a relationship when He put all people in families. Every adult in those little boys' lives took the time to hug and kiss them, contributing to their sense of self-worth. Instead of feeling unloved and rejected, those little boys are growing up with the idea that they are important because everyone important to them loves them.

The Church: Your Substitute Family

One of the vital roles of a good church is to provide a substitute family for the uprooted. At least that is usually the way it works for those who become active and attend regularly enough to make lasting relationships. And if they obey the scriptural admonition to "be given to hospitality," before long the void of resident grandparents and other relatives is filled by other loving adults to whom young children become important. Rarely is that possible for non-Christian families who become victims of urbanization.

Notes

1. Alvin Toffler, *Future Shock* (New York: Random House, 1970), pp. 66, 67.
2. *Ibid.*, p. 85.

10

Easy Divorce

"At least one-third of the divorces that I have granted could have been avoided if they had sought counseling before coming before me," stated a judge who had specialized in marital problems for twenty years.

With the divorce level in 1980 bursting through the 1,150,000 mark, making marriage a fifty–fifty calculated risk and forcing 45 million or so children to spend some portion of their first eighteen years with one parent, something needs to be done to rescue marriage.

Historically marriage has been the cornerstone of the family. And I have found that happily married people do a better job of raising children than do the miserably married. But don't conclude that all of today's happily marrieds were always that way. Many who are celebrating their twenty-fifth anniversaries were in severe conflict in their earlier years, but for religious reasons or to protect their children from the trauma of division, they worked through their problems.

Unfortunately the emphasis today is on making divorce easy or comfortable. California features no-fault divorce, so no one need be embarrassed or even be forced to give reasons for the decision. A judge in San Diego specializes in group divorce, he once granted sixteen divorces simultaneously.

At one time, in California, there was a one-year waiting period between the filing date and the finalization date (each state establishes its own period). When the legislature sought to lower the waiting period to six months, I opposed it vigorously, predicting that it would double the divorce rate in a single decade. I lost, along with thousands of California's children. And sad to say, my prophecy has come true. In fact the rate has more than doubled. Many of the couples who traversed this "easy way out" could have made it had they sought Christian counseling. The unbiblical advice given by some Christians to couples in trouble is appalling. People in the world may adopt the easy-divorce philosophy that emanates from humanistic psychology, but Christians must avoid those lines of reasoning at all costs. Many Christians have unwittingly deferred to humanistic counseling that came from a fellow Christian, only to suffer the consequences later.

Christian counseling is really a misnomer. Many Christians who serve as psychologists, psychiatrists, pastoral counselors, or even church counselors duplicate the advice dispensed by their non-Christian humanistic counterparts. Remember, Christian counseling is much more than counseling with a born-again psychologist. Keep in mind that in order to earn a PhD in psychology, one must have at least 134 hours of graduate studies in humanistic psychology, including the study of Freud, Skinner, Berne, Rogers, and others who are basically anti-Bible. That is why much so-called Christian counseling is little more than humanistic psychology in a Christian environment, administered by a Christian who deletes the swear words and flagrant anti-moral ideas, but still conveys humanistic reasoning. True Christian counseling is biblical counseling, based on God's absolute principles as found in His Word. Such counseling will not convey advice that contradicts the Scriptures.

Some of the guidance that people have repeated to me, administered by Christian counselors, is all but unbelievable. For example, a couple with three children, married thirteen years, was given a battery of psychological tests by a Christian psychologist. According to his report, "Our findings indicate that you are so hopelessly mismatched that you ought to get a divorce." That is a humanistic, not a Christian deduction. The Bible says, "You that are married, seek not to be loosed" (*see* 1 Corinthians 7:27).

Divorce for the Children's Sake?

"It will be better for the children when we get a divorce," pleaded one maritally troubled father of two. That popularized notion is often nothing more than the adults' veiled excuse to justify running from a difficult situation. They salve their consciences by claiming that their decision is "for the good of the children." Divorce is contrary to God's plan, and only in rare and extreme cases is it better for the children.

Dr. Harold Voth, psychiatrist of the Menninger Clinic, points out in his book *The Castrated Family*, that the wisdom of staying together "for the children's sake" is being replaced by "getting divorced for the children's sake," usually to the detriment of the children. Granted, children are brutalized when parents fight and argue, but many times the separation of the child from one of the parents he loves leaves lasting psychic scars. Dr. Voth projects two frequent results for such children:

1. An excessive psychic vulnerability, which makes it harder for them to cope with the normal difficulties of life.

2. Greater difficulty with trust and love within his own family
unit upon entering into adulthood.

The research of Dr. Onalee McGraw is pertinent here.

> Wallerstein and Kelly discuss the findings of their own long-term
> research on 131 divorced families in the San Francisco Bay area.
> Five years after the divorce, 37 percent of the youngsters involved
> were suffering from depression that was manifested in the following:
> chronic and pronounced unhappiness, sexual promiscuity, delin-
> quency in the form of drug abuse, petty stealing, alcoholism and
> acts of breaking and entering, poor learning, intense anger, apathy,
> restlessness, and a sense of intense, unremitting neediness.
> Their study found another 29 percent of the children who were
> making what they described as "appropriate developmental
> progress" but who "continued to experience intermittently a sense
> of deprivation and feelings of sadness and resentment toward one or
> both parents." Thirty-four percent of the youngsters seemed to be
> doing well or comparable to children from intact families after the
> initial breakup. In their study, they found that 56 percent of the
> children surveyed did not consider their post-divorce family to be
> an improvement over their pre-divorce household.[1]

The family is the primary educational source for the teaching of
those human qualities most needed to enjoy one's full potential in
life: love, trust, integrity, self-acceptance, self-sufficiency, responsibility, industry, sharing, and so on. They are best taught in the
home of one's natural parents. If they are at all normal, parents will
love a child more than anyone else. Some stepparents have done an
admirable job as surrogate parents, but few are an improvement
over the original, usually because of the rage, guilt, and self-rejection a child feels when his parents divorce.

I am convinced that death is easier for a child to handle than divorce. When my father died, I experienced traumatic grief for a
while. But even at ten years of age I could understand that my
thirty-four-year-old father could suddenly die from a heart attack,
without rejecting me as a person. I often consoled myself with the
thought, *If dad had a choice, he would be with us.* The child of
divorce has no such means of assurance. I predict that today's
easy-divorce practices will result in a whole generation of psycho-

logically wounded adults who, when entering the marriageable stage in life, will be incapable of giving selfless love to either their partners or their children, thus compounding current tragedies. The only remedy for such psychic scars is a vital spiritual experience that floods such an individual's heart with an abundance of God's love, which he in turn may share with others.

A Tragic Case History

Dr. Mary Calderone is an amazingly talented woman. For almost twenty years this grandmotherly looking woman, wife of the former president of the World Health Organization, has worked tirelessly to introduce our modern youth to the joys of promiscuous sex, which she calls "sexual activity." For a number of years she was the Executive Director of SIECUS (Sex Information and Education Council of the United States) and a Planned Parenthood advocate. As a result of her efforts, radical sex education has been adopted by most of the nation's public junior and senior high schools. Radical sex education is basically explicit sex information without benefit of moral values. In most cases it is hostile to traditional family moral values, aggressively questioning and challenging them. In my opinion, through teaching her anti-moral ideas to our nation's sex education teachers, Mary has done more to destroy virtue, modesty, and the sanctity of sex among our youth, making immorality, teenage pregnancy, and venereal disease almost common in the teenager's quest for "sexual activity," than any other person.

In *The Battle for the Mind,* I indicated that her motivation was religious zeal. That is, Mary is a humanist (recipient of the Humanist of the Year Award for 1974), and humanist educators have been trying for at least two decades to create such an obsession with sex in the minds of our youth that they have no time or interest in spiritual pursuits. Dr. Onalee McGraw's research has uncovered another possibility.

> Parents who fall into divorce because marriage has not reached their "expectations" may be persuaded to be more morally responsible if they realize that by their actions they may impose life-long psychic damage on their children.

Healthy family life produces people who have positive qualities of loyalty, vitality, industriousness, perseverance, courage and integrity. Many parents who undergo divorce and separation work very hard to make up for the loss and to help their children's development in a conscious way. Yet, when the vital love and nurturing is withdrawn through a traumatic loss such as divorce, the rage of a deprived childhood is reaped in later life.

Mary Calderone, former head of Planned Parenthood and Executive Director of SIECUS ... endured such a rejection in her childhood. Mary Calderone's father was the photographer Edward Steichen, famous for his photographs of people all over the world in "The Family of Man" exhibit. Mary Calderone's mother left the family, taking Mary's sister with her and leaving Mary with her father, who farmed her out to the care of various friends. She says about this period in her life: "What insecurities I had arose from the fact that my mother had removed herself from me at a very early age—my parents were separated—and I had no real home. I was sort of farmed out, and even though it was to loving friends, it made me very insecure emotionally.... But I never doubted that someday I would find what I wanted to do and do it."

What Mary Calderone did in her adult life was to promote her vision of the new sexual orthodoxy of self-fulfillment. Is it really surprising that someone as intelligent and determined as this woman would overcome the painful withdrawal of parental love in childhood by proclaiming the message that sexuality is more important than familial values?[2]

Dr. McGraw concludes, "G. K. Chesterton once said, 'He who hates the family does also hate mankind,' to which it might be added, those who are denied the love and nurturing that God intended the family to give may grow up to take their revenge on mankind."[3]

Could it be that some of our social-change agents, masquerading as schoolteachers, government social workers, or youth authorities are driven by similar tragedies? Somehow we must communicate to our generation that marriage is the legitimate doorway to parenthood and that though it doesn't take any skill, character, or self-denial to become a parent, it does to become a good one. We must likewise communicate that while easy divorce is a legal way out, it is neither legitimate with God nor in the best interests of all concerned.

Is Divorce Ever Right?

With millions of single parents struggling valiantly to raise their children in the nurture and admonition of the Lord, I would be remiss not to point out that one legitimate cause for divorce exists. Knowing the lust of mankind and the hardness of the human heart, our Lord taught that there was one exception to "Till death do us part."

Marriage is a legitimate sexual contract that pledges fidelity "so long as we both shall live." Jesus Christ knew that infidelity jeopardized the marriage relationship, and in Matthew 19:5–9 He certified that adultery was a just cause for divorce. Young couples need to know that sexual promiscuity is forbidden by God and is so repugnant to Him that it forms the only basis wherein their partners may legitimately divorce them, placing on them the entire responsibility for the breakup of the marriage.

I have done enough marital counseling to know that there are always two sides to every story, but there is never an excuse for infidelity. First Corinthians 10:13 promises that there will always be "a way of escape." Infidelity may be popular, but it is still wrong. Any Christian married to a promiscuous partner ought to face him or her with the fact of sin. If he or she refuses to repent and desist, divorce proceedings may be instituted, and the injured party may demand a just and adequate financial settlement for the family. I have found that the sooner such action is initiated, the better are the chances for repentance and restoration. But a partner who continues to live with a promiscuous mate opens himself or herself to VD, destruction of self-image, the lies and deceit that always follow sexual sins, and ultimately the judgment of God on the family. Although restoration should be sought, it must be based on genuine repentance.

Once the divorce action has been necessitated by the offending partner, the other should live with a clear conscience toward God, "void of offense," actively seeking God's help in rearing the family and being reponsive to His direction toward their future. God, who is "a father of the fatherless," will supply the family's basic needs, not only physically, but spiritually and emotionally.

Notes

1. Onalee McGraw, *The Family, Feminism and the Therapeutic State* (Washington, D.C.: The Heritage Foundation, 1980), p. 24.
2. *Ibid,* pp. 25, 26.
3. *Ibid,* p. 26.

11

Women in the Work Force

According to a recent magazine report:

Women are swelling the work force at a rate of almost 2 million every year—a phenomenon that is beginning to transform everyday life in the United States.

They have left the home and taken jobs in numbers once unimagined. In the process, females have shattered traditional barriers against them in many occupations.

From astronaut to zoologist, nearly every occupation has been invaded by women, who are pouring into the job market almost twice as fast as men. More than half the country's 84 million women, including a majority of mothers with school-age children, now work or seek jobs.

So dramatic is the shift from homemaking to careers that Eli Ginzberg, head of the National Commission for Manpower Policy, describes it as "bigger than the atomic bomb or nuclear power."

Ginzberg predicts that the desire of women for jobs ultimately may alter the lives of every American. "It changes the relationship of men to women; it changes the relationship of mothers to children. And the future of the suburbs may also be in doubt."

The working woman appears to be playing a key role in a wave of social change that includes return of middle-class families to the cities, fewer children, later marriages, more divorces and longer life expectancy.

For the working woman herself, a job means independence, a sense of accomplishment and—most important—money.[1]

By contrast, a 1980 Gallup survey concerning working women indicated that 74 percent of the nation's women "choose a marriage with children as the most interesting and satisfying life for themselves."[2] With all the emphasis on women's lib, female rights, and self-assertiveness for women, during this decade, Gallup indicated that the percentage was virtually unchanged from four years earlier. He further stated, "Relatively few women, only 7%, prefer to remain single, free and occupied with a full-time career. These women are likely to be college-educated, ages 18–34, and living in the West."[3]

The working mother is not a recent phenomenon! Women, like men, have always worked. In fact, though it pains me somewhat to admit it, my travels in forty-four countries of the world and on every continent convince me that women have historically worked longer and harder than men. I still cannot rid from my mind the sight of women in Mexico, South America, Africa, and India, who carried large and often heavy loads on their backs and heads while their husbands sauntered ahead of them, carrying little more than walking sticks. Interestingly enough, the men always explained, "In the old days there were enemies in the bush and the husband had to be prepared at all times to defend the womenfolk." For some reason they seem unwilling to help carry the load, now that marauding tribes no longer infest the jungle—much as modern husbands still have difficulty helping with home chores, now that 60 percent of the married American women work out of the home and still attend to their duties as homemakers.

No, work is not the issue. But the fact that many married women work outside the home is a phenomenon unique to the twentieth century.

At the beginning of World War I, approximately 4 percent of the work force was made up of women, and many of these were schoolteachers. Because teaching the young was considered an extension of the home and the rightful duty of women, in the nineteenth century, 80 percent of all schoolteachers were women. In fact the pay scale for public-school teachers was so low that few men, particularly family heads, chose it as a profession.

Until 1914 "a woman's place was in the home." Then the necessities of war forced many women to join the work force outside the home and inaugurate a trend that today includes almost 40 million women, just 25 million less than the number of men who work. As the commercial says, "You've come a long way, baby"; but many overworked women, wives, and mothers are beginning to ask, "Is it really worth it?"

Why Women Are Seeking Jobs

In a day when more children come home from school to empty houses than to cheery hellos from mom and snacks of cookies and milk, we must ask ourselves: *Why do almost 60 percent of America's mothers seek jobs?* As one would expect, the reasons are multiple. Here are four.

1. The Feminist Emphasis We have already felt the harmful impact of the feminist movement, as a few noisy, self-appointed, and often hostile women (led primarily by humanists) have deceived the press, educators, government bureaucrats, and many others into thinking that they speak for the women of America. Actually, they represent only themselves, thousands of lesbians, and the deceived followers who are unaware of their true goals. But because the rest of us were asleep in the mid-sixties and throughout the seventies, they almost succeeded in changing the whole image of womanhood.

Feminist educators have used the threat of "sexism" to force school textbooks and teaching aids to deemphasize motherhood, homemaking, fatherhood, and masculinity, until girls who desire to be feminine and aspire to become homemakers are made to feel second-rate. Motherhood is the greatest calling in the world, according to God; He honored Eve in giving her a name meaning "mother of all living" (Genesis 3:20). But our children's school texts reflect just the opposite. Children growing up in a school and social environment in which women are given strong identities as telephone repair persons or locomotive engineers can hardly be expected to aspire to homemaking—to their own peril.

The feminist emphasis in newspaper reporting has had no small impact on formulating the ideals of today's womanhood. A journalist, during an interview with my wife, clearly defined her bias by saying, "The family is not *really* as important as it used to be. With all the modern agencies to instruct, assist, and guide individuals today, it doesn't matter anymore whether a person has a strong family background." It is such well-advertised thinking that has caused girls to think career instead of homemaking and has largely delayed their marriage and motherhood plans until age thirty or more. This has likewise contributed to today's family of 1.6 children. Fortunately there seems to be a growing reaction to all this artificial family emphasis, which may well result in a backlash of "Let's hear it for motherhood and the housewife!" Gradually the women of America are awakening to the realization that the feminist movement is not based on traditional moral values. Therefore those who wish to live in a moral culture should refrain from adopting feminist rhetoric and theories.

2. Increased Skills and Education of Women   During the past few years we have witnessed an enormous increase in the number of women who attend college, both undergraduate and graduate school. Marriage immediately after high school is not nearly so prevalent as it once was. Consequently, young women lean toward seeking careers, learning skills, or going to college. With 9 percent more women in the country than men, many women feel that post-high-school training is a matter of survival. The doubling of the divorce rate in the past decade, making a successful marriage a fifty-fifty chance at best, has stirred many women to establish a realistic career goal, "just in case."

3. Decrease in Hard Labor Tasks   Ever since machinery began to replace manual labor, men have consistently reduced the need to earn their "bread by the sweat of their face." While it is still true that man generally has forty to eighty more pounds of upper-body strength than his female counterpart, very few jobs still require it (except construction, in which we continue to have fewer women in the work force).

4. Increased Technology   Many researchers who list the differences between men and women indicate that their tests show women by nature better equipped than may men to run certain kinds of sophisticated machinery and electronic devices. Women tend to have greater manual dexterity than the average man. Consequently, future technology favors greater numbers of women entering the work force. The twenty-first century may find the number of women working outside the home equal to that of men. Maternity is the only phenomenon that may keep that prediction from becoming a reality, and medical science and planned parenthood are working feverishly on that.

5. Economic Necessity   Women are leaving the kitchen to work outside the home today out of economic necessity—as they see it. Surveys show that the largest number of working women come from the lowest income brackets. Other studies indicate that only 30 percent of today's women really want to leave the home, and many of those do not want their positions to be permanent. According to an authority on family finances, only 7 to 10 percent of all working women report that they have taken a job for personal fulfillment. Why, then, do the others work? Out of necessity.

Many Christian women work today to provide the tuition money necessary to send their children to Christian schools. Usually they wait until the youngest child is in his teen years, when the humanistic philosophy of the public schools becomes so acute that mothers can find no alternative. Unfortunately the new emphasis of the schools in starting radical sex education while children are still in kindergarten and first grade is forcing even more of these mothers into the labor market.

Is 12 Percent Enough?

Working women throughout the Western world are coming to the sad realization that by the time they have paid the additional costs of transportation, higher-income and social-security taxes, tithes, union dues, clothing, lunch, and particularly child care, they only gain 12 to 30 percent by working forty hours a week outside their home. Because their efforts put such a strain on the whole family, many are beginning to take a second look at it and ask, "Is it really worth it?"

Perhaps we should more deeply evaluate the problems generated by working wives and mothers to see if, indeed, it is worth the price—even if it provided a 100 percent gain, which it never does.

No matter how capable she is, a wife has only so much time in any given week—assuming that working hours, including transportation to and from work plus lunch hours, encompass the prime hours of 7:00 A.M. to 5:30 P.M. (that's approximately 52 hours each week). To perform well, at least five days per week she will need to expend physical energy, mental creativity, and concentration for other than family duties during that priority time. Examined from another perspective, the average person has only 112 waking hours per week. A single woman can afford to spend 52 of those hours outside the home, but a wife and mother is sorely pressed to sacrifice that many hours to her home responsibilities. By the time she adds her vocational hours as wife and as mother of one or more children, she can reserve little or no waking time for herself. As a family counselor for thirty years, I find that such a strain on a marriage and home should never be imposed, unless absolutely necessary. But even time pressures are not the only dangers to the working family woman. Consider these three:

1. *It Is a Threat to a Marriage* While modern appliances and push-button gadgetry have greatly simplified homemaking, time and energy factors do not account for all the stress on a marriage when the wife works out of the home, particularly if she works full-time. There is a realistic danger that a family will create an unrealistic standard of living on two incomes and then attempt to make it a permanent way of life. At the risk of sounding chauvinistic, I should point out that it also has a tendency to make many young wives very independent, and this may have two serious drawbacks for young couples. First, the new husband may feel insecure. I realize that such a potential fails to impress the feminists, but it is a fact of life that most young men embark upon a marriage with feelings of insecurity about their abilities to properly lead their wives. If a wife earns almost as much as her husband, that could threaten his self-acceptance in his new role as provider and protector of his home. Additionally, that second income, inducing a spirit of independence, may inhibit the wife's feeling of dependence on her husband, particularly in times of marital tension (and every good marriage experiences some of those, especially in the early years). It is far better at such times, as the Bible teaches, that "her desire shall be to her husband." That does not admonish her to be his slave, but that she look to him rather than to her own self-sufficiency for provision and sustenance. The divorce rate, which is higher for working than for nonworking wives, is evidence that the feeling and opportunity for independence makes divorce an excessively easy option, to the disadvantage of both. Even when the independent income does not accelerate the possibility of divorce, it tends to increase the degree of conflict.

2. *It Is a Threat to the Family* We have already noted that the home is supposed to be family members' haven from the pressures of a competitive and often hostile world. It is extremely difficult for that home to become such a haven unless someone, preferably an adult, is there to produce the necessary atmosphere. Almost every working mother will admit that arriving from work around dinner time puts her behind schedule, and she rarely catches up before bedtime. Being a full-time careerist, for a woman, will often come at the expense of her natural desire to supply the needs of her home, unless she receives a great deal of support from her husband and children. This is one reason so many wives wait until their children are in junior- or senior-high school to commence work. It also explains why so many women are stopping with only two children.

Husbands have generally been slow to voluntarily share the household responsibilities and chores with their working spouses. They often expect the same service from their working partners that they received when they stayed at home as resident domestic engineers. They remember enjoying early dinners, relaxation, and paper; romping with the children before bedtime; sharing a backrub, pillowtalk, and regular loving. I have long wondered whether the life span for women—four years longer than for men— is really true for America's working women.

3. It Is a Threat to Young Children   In recent years the career woman has tended to carry her baby through the eighth month of a rigorous work schedule, deliver the child, and within two months return to work. Contemporary research suggests that such a procedure may be harmful to both the mother and the infant. Chicago *Tribune* women's writer Joan Beck asks:

> Would mothers of very young children be willing to work full time outside the home if they knew it could lower their youngsters intelligence measurably? . . .
> Evidence continues to pile up that the role a mother plays in the life of her child during the first three years of life has a crucial, lasting effect on his intelligence. And the components of this relationship include critical elements which cannot easily be supplied by mother substitutes or day-care centers. . . .
> Newest bits of evidence linking a young child's intelligence with the quality of mothering and the amount of mental stimulation in the home comes from the Journal of Educational Psychology. It reports new studies showing that for both black and white youngsters, the quality of early home life is much more closely related to mental test scores later on than such other factors as socio-economic status.

Earlier research by the same team (Robert H. Bradley and Bettye Caldwell of the University of Arkansas at Little Rock and Richard Elardo, University of Missouri–St. Louis) has been aimed at pinpointing precisely what it is in the home environment that affects I.Q.—for better or for worse.

Most important elements include the mother's involvement with the child, the verbal and emotional responsiveness of the mother and the provision of appropriate materials, this research shows. Also important are opportunities for variety in daily routines, the avoidance of restrictions and punishment, and the organization of learning opportunities in the home.

These findings on the effects of early learning and mothering back up other continuing studies on babies and toddlers at Harvard and elsewhere. All show consistently that intelligence, competence, and creativity develop best when a young child has plenty of stimulating things to do and a mother nearby to keep feeding him appropriate words almost continually.

It isn't the kind of mothering you can concentrate into a grudging, tired hour after a full day of work outside the home. It needs to be spread out over the waking day of the baby or toddler, keyed to his immediate interests and carefully matched to his responses and level of development.[4]

The above survey only cites the intellectual damage to a small child who does not have the benefit of a mother's constancy. Someday a research team may report the emotional difficulties that arise in early childhood when a youngster grows up without benefit of the working mother's presence throughout much of the day. I predict this trend will produce millions of future adults who have problems with self-image, emotional security, depression, and hostility—a high price to pay for working, unless it is absolutely necessary.

The danger is not lost on today's young women either.

In a recent study by Brown University of 3,000 college students at Barnard, Brown, Dartmouth, Princeton, Wellesley and the State University of New York at Stony Brook, L.I., 77 percent of the women said mothers should either not work at all or work only part-time until their children were 5. Eighty four percent of the men agreed. . . .

While some said that they would entrust their youngsters to housekeepers or day-care centers, many said they found this option unacceptable because in their limited experience the children of working mothers were not so well-adjusted as those raised by mothers who stayed at home.[5]

I find it gratifying that many young college women are seeing through the feminist movement, which has agitated careerism, regardless of the cost, based on its humanist commitment to self-actualization. Perhaps those women who really want to be mothers more than they desire careers will wake up to the fact that they are in the majority. If that ever happens, motherhood may again become fashionable.

Notes

1. "Working Women: Joys and Sorrows," *U.S. News & World Report* 87 (15 January 1979), p. 64.
2. "Women's Ideal Lifestyle," *Parade Magazine,* 28 December 1980, p. 9.
3. *Ibid.*
4. Joan Beck, "Mothers May Have To Weigh Job Vs. Tot I.Q.," *Fort Worth Star-Telegram,* 11 April 1978, p. 3B.
5. "Coeds Face Quandary: Family or Career?" *San Diego Union,* 2 January 1981, p. A-14.

12

Pornography: Mental Poison

Throughout the nation violent rape, child molestation, sexploitation of children, homophilia, sadomasochism, perversion, and even sex murders have been increasing at an alarming rate during the

past decade. During the same period of time, pornographic literature has burst into a $5 billion business in America.

"Two hundred seventy magazines deal with sex filth," reported
Attorney Charles H. Keating, Jr., head of Citizens for Decency
Through Law. These magazines "glorify child molesting, rape and
gang orgies. There are films and videotapes which outdo the ancient
Greeks and Romans in depicting pagan perversion." Slick periodicals and films contain telephoto scenes of every conceivable pose
which the perverted minds of pornographers can conceive. With a
two-dollar price tag for smut hustlers like *Playboy* and *Penthouse,* it
is twice as profitable to the distributors as *Time, Life,* and *Saturday
Evening Post.*

Many of the most shocking crimes today are inspired when
morally sick words and living-color pictures are transmitted,
through the printing press, into an equally sick mind, arousing the
individual to horrifying action. We will not halt this sordid, sex-
crazed crime rate until we rid our nation of pornography in magazines, X-rated and "adult" movies, and particularly "kiddie porn."
As sick as it may seem, over 5,000 child molesters in Los Angeles
devotedly read kiddie porn, even though the use of children in such
poses is against the law. In a distorted application of "freedom of
speech" (which is taken to mean freedom to read and freedom from
censorship), who can be certain that his child is protected?

A couple in our church called for counseling. I had performed
their marriage ceremony and dedicated their four-year-old girl. The
reason for their call: Their daughter had been molested by a neighbor. Investigation showed that he was a porno reader with a fascination for kiddie porn. If proper investigation were made, I am
confident that pornographic literature and movies would be declared the prime causes of today's sex crimes.

As I have shown in previous books, the emotions serve as the
motor of man. These emotions (or heart) are responsive to the
thoughts we maintain in our minds, and the most effective assault
on the mind is through the eyes. Consequently we artificially inflame our emotions by reading or seeing sexually inflammatory
material.

Pornography Is Antifamily

It is easy to make a case for the fact that modern pornography in all its sophisticated forms is harmful to the family. My counseling experience suggests that it causes couples to commence a marriage with unnatural expectations. This is even more true when only one is a porn user. How can a chaste, modest wife measure up to the fiendish fantasies in the mind of her porn-reading bridegroom? She may perform 100 percent normally, but return from her honeymoon feeling inadequate, dirty, and used. The scenes in pornographic literature are anything but normal. And the problem is not limited to the young. Some couples have written our Counseling by Mail ministry or have sought counseling, due to sexual strife, after twenty-five years of marriage. We have determined that the unfulfilled expectations cited could not have been conceived in a normal brain, but were passed on by professional perverters called pornographers. I would judge that fully two-thirds of the sexual problems in marriage today can be traced to the use of pornography.

The Bible, which is very clear on this subject, condemns it in no uncertain terms.

> But fornication and all uncleanness or covetousness, let it not even be named among you, as is fitting for saints; neither filthiness, nor foolish talking, nor coarse jesting, which are not fitting. . . . And have no fellowship with the unfruitful works of darkness, but rather expose them. For it is shameful even to speak of those things which are done by them in secret.
>
> Ephesians 5:3, 4, 11, 12 NKJV–NT

Teens Are Extremely Vulnerable

No teenager will ever profit from an obsession with sex. Boys particularly need to steer clear of anything visually inflammatory. As their bodies go through the process of development, they are extremely excited by lewd pictures. At a time when they should be channeling their energies into academic and athletic interests or learning to work with their hands, it is very harmful for them to gain easy access to pornography, which captivates their imaginations and supersedes all other thoughts. For most young boys it serves to destroy the beauty of sex and reduce it to a base level. Femininity is stripped of its mystique, and in its place girls are fantasized as objects of lust, to be used at will. Instead of placing girls on pedestals of respect that used to incite young men to protect a girl's modesty and virtue, porn users find it easy to spew foul language in the company of the opposite sex and offend girls with dirty jokes or suggestive remarks. Nice girls are repulsed by porn users.

Pornography, of course, is not limited to boys. It also corrupts the morals of girls and sears their sensibilities. But due to a psychological difference between men and women, it is more harmful to boys than girls. Women who use pornography are usually well down the road to depravity. Unless introduced to it through their sex education courses in school or through a friend, most girls don't seek it out. Although a few pornographic magazines have appeared for women, the big users are men.

Jack Palmer, a supervisory counselor in Juvenile Hall in San Diego for twenty-five years, is a personal friend and a member of the church I serve. To my question, "What percentage of the young men in Juvenile Hall are pornography users?" he responded, "Over 90 percent." Then I asked, "What about juvenile sex offenders?" He replied, "Virtually all of them!"

Authorities and parents fail to realize that pornography affects a person much like drugs and alcohol. Just as drugs artificially excite the emotions (up or down), making a person feel good or bad, hostile or passive, pornography passing through the eye into the brain can artificially inflame a person to sexual arousal.

On the last day of 1980, a seventy-six-year-old former Hollywood actress was attacked in her home by a seventeen-year-old who had been released from juvenile confinement for a "holiday furlough" to see if he was ready to be paroled into society. According to her testimony, he grabbed her and said, "I don't want to hurt or rob you; all I want is sex!" Had she not been able to pick up a claw hammer and strike him between the eyes, he would have raped her. Whom do you blame for such a tragedy? The humanistically trained psychiatrist who recommended his early release? The liberal-minded (humanist) parole board that seems more interested in "rehabilitating criminals" than in protecting the innocent taxpayers? The pornographers who publish and distribute the smut that so inflamed his mind that he was willing to attack a woman old enough to be his grandmother? The five United States Supreme Court members who voted to make such printed filth easily accessible? The parents who did not teach their son to purify his mind and failed to block his access to lewd or suggestive literature and fellowship with youths with similar values? All share the responsibility for such crime; but the courageous old woman, the pathetic teenager, and society are the victims.

It Can Happen to You!

Don't protest that such a nightmare can't happen to you or your family. I know better, and in your heart so do you. Your family is not any more exempt from such tragedy than the Christian couple who came to me heartbroken when their nineteen-year-old daughter admitted that she had left home the year before to become a prostitute. Naturally the couple asked, "Where did we go wrong?" At fifteen their daughter was a sweet, innocent girl who regularly attended church with them. They did note her peculiar associations with the "out of it" group at church, but they prayed she would come around. Investigation revealed that at sixteen she had started having sex with a boyfriend. He invited her and three other couples to the home of a friend whose parents worked during the day. The boy distributed his father's *Playboy* magazines, and they all began reading them until they got so worked up that they stripped off their clothes and performed sexual acts in front of each other. This was followed by sex orgies, until their daughter had run the gamut of sexual experience by the time she was seventeen. Depravity never happens suddenly. It is a progressive process, but nothing speeds a normal person's decency into the maelstrom of indecency faster than pornography.

The Decency-in-Literature Amendment

This country needs an amendment to our federal Constitution that will permit law-enforcement officials to close down smut peddlers and stop this very profitable and corrupting business. It won't be easy, of course, because $5 billion provides them sufficient incentive and political buying power to hire the best pornographic lawyers in the country. In fact, some who specialize in this field of law may volunteer their services just to keep from losing their high-paying clients. That is why a decency-in-literature amendment is the one way to put teeth into our laws. It should be carefully prepared so as not to violate reasonable rights under the First Amendment, but we need to protect our families from this vile scourge.

The moment we mention decency in literature, guaranteed either by amendment or legislation, hypocritical cries of "Censorship" are raised by pornographers and their humanist friends. That is merely a smoke screen. We have laws that protect our citizens from poisoning each other; we prohibit prostitution; speed limits are legislated; compulsory education, taxation, safety, and pollution standards are mandated; even cigarettes must carry the surgeon general's warning that smoking is dangerous to one's health, and tobacco-industry advertising has been legally dropped from TV. Why not protect the minds of our citizens (and particularly our children) from the corrupting effects of pornography? With all due respect to the importance of clean lungs, it is far more important to have a clean mind, for the brain is the most important organ in the body.

The humanist ACLU lawyer from Texas who has defended more pornography publishers than any other was interviewed on a TV talk show. I found his arguments quite interesting. Like all pornography defenders, he immediately declared that we must protect the First Amendment guarantee of free speech and press. According to his philosophy, anything that limits that is "worse than pornography." He then pointed out that the antipornography movement is dangerous because it would "legalize morality." After further questioning, however, he surprisingly indicated that he opposed kiddie porn as despicable and illegal, claiming he would not defend a kiddie-porn publisher.

This man's testimony simply illustrates that we *must* legalize morality to some degree or be doomed to live in filth. Why would he legislate against kiddie porn, but not adult porn? Why does the former violate the First Amendment, but not the latter? Because he says so! Frankly we have just as much right as the humanists to set the standards of morality, particularly since we represent the overwhelming majority of the population in this country. The real difference between us (though the humanists will not admit it) is not whether a society must legislate morality, but *where* the lines are set. Even humanists know that we have consistently used the legislative process to protect morality, as in our laws against stealing, rape, perjury, and murder. We differ, however, on the issue of sexual practices. Some humanists even want to legalize incest, which is unthinkable to anyone committed to traditional moral values.

Simply stated, the laws of our country prohibit indecent exposure, public nudity, child molesting, intercourse between an adult and minor, and many other activities. Any literature or film that portrays such illegal sex acts should likewise be declared pornographic and outlawed. The fines for such offenses should be multiple. For example, each time a publisher is fined for the same offense, the penalty should be doubled. Currently the fine is so low and pornography is so profitable that many pornography publishers gladly pay the modest penalties out of their profits.

Personally I look for a ground swell of reaction to pornography that will soon demand that our elected leaders protect us from this plague. Women in particular will raise voices of protest, for it is gradually dawning on them that the frightening rise in rape statistics is primarily due to two things: pornography and leniency on rapists.

I am convinced that the elimination of pornography from America would reduce forcible rape by 30 to 40 percent, and stiffer and faster penalties for rapists would cut it another 30 to 40 percent. It is just a matter of time before one of our Moral Majority organizations or our pro-moral senators put together a well-organized campaign to outlaw it. Together with outraged and fearful women throughout the country, we will succeed in putting pornographers out of business. The streets of America should gradually become safe for unescorted women, day or night. That is a right that should be guaranteed by our Constitution. The present lenient laws on pornography discriminate against that natural right of womanhood.

Until such a law or amendment is passed, parents must be vigilant to see that their children are not being secretly polluted by the cesspool of pornography.

13

Free Access to Drugs

My doctor friend had tears in his eyes when I entered his office. To my inquiry "What's the matter?" he replied, "Did you notice the young man who just left? I delivered that boy, and I watched him

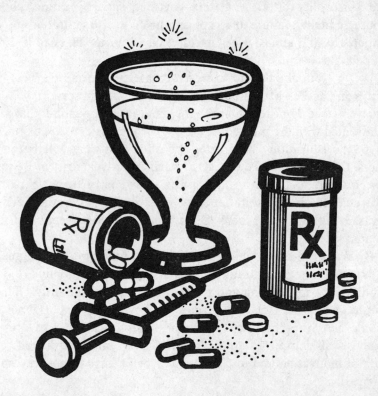

grow up. He was a straight-A student and was given a scholarship to Stanford University, where he got hooked on drugs. For five years he was strung out so bad that he couldn't finish college. In fact, he used to sit on a rock down by the ocean and strum his guitar by the hour. Six months ago I led him to Christ and helped him kick the drug habit. Today we went over his latest medical report, which confirmed my suspicions: He has permanent brain damage!" Thanks to our humanist educators, government bureaucrats, and judges, a lad who inherited an IQ of close to 150 will struggle the rest of his life to keep a job.

It is impossible for me to be objective when it comes to drugs. As a family counselor for many years, I have observed it heap devastating heartache on families. I have watched its effects in changing the personality or value system—causing spouse beating, child abuse, infidelity, failure to accept responsibility, unnatural hostility, impotence, and almost every harmful consequence that can be imagined.

It is all but impossible to overestimate the harmful effects of drugs on families. Measured in the light of human misery, only God knows its true damage. You probably know several families that are confronted with the problem. The longer their children are exposed to public education, the greater the odds that they will become users. Dr. D. Harvey Powelson, a practicing psychiatrist in Berkeley, California, formerly chief of the psychiatry department of Cowell Memorial Hospital at the University of California, Berkeley, said of the students there, ". . . around 80 to 90 percent use marijuana."[1]

By *drugs* I mean anything that alters the function of the human mind, anything that will foment a change in personality due to the modification in thinking and feeling produced by the drugs. That would include alcohol, barbiturates, "downers" or "uppers," marijuana, heroin, opium, LSD, and the other so-called hard drugs. They are all detrimental to the family. Their symptoms range from lack of motivation and loss of memory or feelings to hostility and aggression.

Drugs have an impact on the family unlike any of the other

harmful forces I am reviewing in this book. Why? Because they alter the function, thinking, and values of the human brain. In fact, they are so dangerous, yet commonplace, that they almost seem to provide an exception to Proverbs 22:6. There the wise man said, "Train up a child in the way he should go: and when he is old, he will not depart from it." The mind-destroying potential of drugs can nullify that promise by keeping a young person from living long enough to get old.

The enormity of current drug traffic, making it accessible to almost every young person, does not even make the child raised properly exempt. That is why every young person must know the full story on drugs, from a Christian perspective, for even a single dose can destroy his life. We are familiar with the tragedy that befell the Art Linkletter family when their beautiful twenty-one-year-old daughter took LSD and, thinking she could fly, stepped out a fourth-story window, to her death. What parent today can say with any degree of certainty, "That could never happen to my child"?

I have even known of cases when drugs were administered to young people without their knowledge. *Reader's Digest* carried the story of a jet pilot who was court-martialed for taking angel dust (PCP). Due only to the persistence of his squadron leader, Commander Lonnie McClung, a member of our church, the pilot was exonerated. Lonnie knew the lad and was convinced that he would never knowingly jeopardize his flying career by taking drugs. Through dogged determination he pursued the investigation and discovered that the young officer's clothing had somehow been stored with some other passenger's clothes containing the powerful dust, and thus his uniform had become contaminated. Every time he put those clothes on, his behavior became so bizarre that he was hospitalized. It was finally discovered that the drug was so embedded in the seams of his trousers and shirt that even washing did not remove it. Fortunately, only one uniform was contaminated, but just having the drug against his skin altered the function of his brain.[2]

Our government, which is supposed to protect the families of our country from such potential tragedies, is failing to help.

... the volume of illicit drugs entering the country is sharply on the rise. Stuart E. Eizenstat, President Carter's domestic-affairs adviser, told congressional leaders that four cities—New York, Newark, Baltimore and Washington, D.C.—"are now experiencing severe problems." He warned of a possible national "heroin epidemic."

Governor Hugh Carey of New York complained in late October that an epidemic of "the pure white stuff" already afflicted his state and the nation.

If the flow of heroin is up, why are drug seizures down? William Green, deputy assistant commissioner in charge of border operations for Customs, says: "It can mean we are doing a lousy job, or it may mean that there simply is no way to stop it at all."[3]

It seems that a bureaucratic reorganization of the Customs Department has all but rendered that agency helpless to stop this increasing menace.

Then, starting about a year ago, the amount of high-quality heroin reaching American cities again reached tidal proportions. Tests show that the new flow of drugs consists of so-called Persian-gold heroin, which comes from strife-torn Iran, Afghanistan and Pakistan. Efforts to curb this supply at the source have run aground.[4]

If federal bureaucrats would use our tax money to protect the family, instead of trying to control it, the quality of family life would be greatly enhanced. Since it will be some time before we expect relief from a conservative government, parents will have to work diligently to protect their youth from these mind-destroying drugs, particularly if they send them to public school, where most young people are first introduced to them.

Marijuana: A Hard Drug

All intelligent parents fear the use of hard drugs, but due to faulty advertising of those who want to legalize marijuana, many think it is little more harmful than cigarettes. My research indicated quite the contrary. Dr. Hardin B. Jones, professor of Medical Physics and Physiology at the University of California, Berkeley, has been fighting the use of marijuana since 1965. Noting that several of his university colleagues advocated its use as "harmless," he began to research the field and today is a leading authority on the subject. He was the first to recoganize that one or two smokes or "joints" may appear harmless, but marijuana tends to accumulate in the system. Five or six in a thirty-day period may have a more powerful effect than just one or two. He states:

> Now we know by careful chemical measurements taken in the bodies of marijuana users that the drug actually accumulates in a linear way.... A week after a person smokes marijuana, 30 percent is still in the body in the active form. There is no other drug or medication that I know of that lingers in the body so long. Of the portion that remains, the body retains 70 percent of that longer than the second week. It gets rid of only 10 percent a month thereafter, so the burden stays in the body for a long period, and as the person uses more and more, it accumulates....
>
> When a young person begins to smoke marijuana, he doesn't get much effect the first few times. But after five or six times, suddenly he gets intoxicated. That happens because enough of the stuff has accumulated in the surface membrane of the brain cells so that it can kick off an intoxicative experience. The body has to have a sufficient accumulation before the user gets that effect.
>
> What is not realized is that the marijuana user is never completely free of some of these low-grade intoxicative effects. The brain makes adjustments to drug burdens. A person can take alcohol or barbiturates or other substances that are intoxicating, and the brain will adapt so that it will get along in spite of the effect.
>
> Likewise, the brains of marijuana users make the best adjustment they can, but they can't get around all the effects. I can see some effects in all marijuana users any time I examine them, even though they haven't used marijuana for hours, days or weeks.[5]

Some of the latest research indicates that even mild marijuana users endanger their brains if they use it regularly. For example, smoking just three joints a week for ten years can cause permanent brain damage, loss of memory, goal disorientation, male sterility, and contamination of the eggs in a woman's ovum. The future children of America are severely threatened by this "relatively harmless drug."

The Alcoholic Epidemic

One popular beer commercial boasts that 11 million cans of their beer are consumed daily in this country alone. The World Health Organization indicates that alcohol consumption has increased at a staggering rate throughout the world. While visiting Russia, just four years ago, we learned that 30 to 40 percent of their hospital beds were occupied by people with alcohol problems.

In America, where over $500 million a year is spent advertising alcohol and beer, hard-liquor consumption increased 85 million gallons between 1969 and 1978, beer consumption 1.5 billion gallons. It is estimated that adults in the United States drank an average of three gallons of hard liquor last year and in excess of 32 gallons of beer. Alcoholism's cost in dollars amounted to 43 billion dollars in 1975. The cost in human suffering and family breakdown is incalculable.

A *Time* survey of 7,000 college students' drinking habits indicated that "95% of the undergraduates report at least occasional drinking. . . . Twenty percent of the men and 10% of the women say getting drunk 'was important' to them. The category of 'heavy drinkers'—those who regularly consume more than a six-pack of beer or five shots of liquor at a sitting—now includes 29% of undergraduate men and 11% of the women." According to the article, "At four Florida universities, 30% of the students polled told researchers they have missed classes because of hangovers."[6]

The reason I include alcohol in the problems of drugs is threefold:

First, alcohol is the first step toward drugs. Experts indicate that most drug users started with alcohol.

Second, alcohol use, which is on an incredible rise in this country, has a mind changing effect on the brain.

Third, although it is forbidden (Ephesians 5:18), it seems to be an increasing fad among Christians, much to their own detriment.

Both my wife and I have noticed that the Christian who starts by drinking wine often proceeds to beer, to hard liquor, and then to other sins. A person does not start with flagrant sin; he works up to it gradually. Wine and beer usually form the first step down the path to what previously was considered unthinkable carnality.

The Mind Set of Drug Users

Among Christians, both youth and adults, we find two interesting parallels in the use of drugs and sexual promiscuity:

1. They both are so contrary to God's plan for one's life that they involve a definite mind set to do wrong. Whenever a young person pops the first pill, he knows he is deliberately violating the law of God. This always leads to a defiant, rebellious attitude that spills over into other areas.
2. The person who takes drugs or gets involved with illicit sex will not hesitate to lie, cheat, steal, or resort to any other sin (except murder) to cover up that sin.

The only remedy for either of these sins is a genuine repentance that involves shame, sorrow, confession, humility, and a surrender of the will to God. Even then it will take the power of God and the loving support of a family or friends to help the person overcome the problem. But the individual will never master his weakness until he reverses the mental decision he made at the start and establishes the mind set of *total abstinence*.

Home Is a Haven

My file contains a letter from a family counselor at a large Marine Corps base near San Diego. "At least 70 percent of the family problems I face daily are drug or alcohol related," he reports. That seems like a high price to pay for "a trip" or "relaxation" or "escape." Taking drugs does not solve problems, but will inevitably compound them.

Never in the history of the world has it been more essential for the family to safeguard each of its members—particularly its young—from drugs such as alcohol and marijuana. The most successful approach is to eliminate all drugs from your home, monitor the children's friends carefully, and teach by example and precept the dangers of drug usage. The father who drinks a six-pack will never convince his children that drugs are harmful.

The Christian's enjoyment is not dependent on liquids, pills, capsules, or joints, but on the living God. Ephesians 5:18 and Galatians 5:22, 23 very clearly teach:

> And do not be drunk with wine, in which is dissipation; but be filled with the Spirit.
>
> Ephesians 5:18 NKJV–NT

> But the fruit of the Spirit is love, joy, peace, longsuffering, kindness, goodness, faithfulness, gentleness, self-control. Against such there is no law.
>
> Galatians 5:22, 23 NKJV–NT

When your home is filled with these blessings, who needs anything more?

Notes

1. D. Harvey Ponelson, *Our Most Dangerous Drug* (Washington, D.C.: Narcotics Education, Inc.).
2. Gerald Moore, "Lieutenant Chmelir's Deadly Wardrobe," *Reader's Digest* 115 (October 1979), pp. 152–57.
3. Orr Kelly, "New Flood of Heroin, and Why It Isn't Stopped," *U.S. News & World Report* 88 (8 December 1980), p. 36.
4. *Ibid.*
5. Hardin B. Jones, "What Marijuana Really Does" (Washington, D.C.: Narcotics Education, Inc.).
6. "Going Back to the Booze," *Time,* 115 (5 November 1979), p. 71.

14

Rock Music

Today one of the most consistent sources of conflict between parents and teens is rock music. Most adults object to the sound, either its beat or its volume. However, the words and message, often un-

intelligible to the parent, are far more harmful. As a parent and pastor, for many years I have long recognized that rock music listening and teenage rebellion went hand in hand. The more a person listens to rock, the more he seems to rebel against both God and man. I do not know any heavy rock listeners who are growing, aggressive Christians.

As a parent, I did not permit rock 'n' roll to become a major in-house problem. Rock concerts, recordings, and movies were not debatable options. Consequently, controversy was kept to a minimum. I have noticed, however, that Christian parents who compromise on this issue often lose the battle in other conflicts.

At lunch one day a mother was so concerned over the problem that she shared this story with my wife, in front of several other mothers. Her fourteen-year-old daughter reminded her continually, with loud protestations, "All the other kids at my Christian school listen to rock music on the radio in their rooms. Why can't I?" Aware of the increasing signs of rebellion in her teen as she plunged into puberty, the mother had decided six months earlier to give in. After all, "Everyone else did it." Bev asked, "Has it made her less rebellious?" The mother admitted sheepishly, "To the contrary, she is worse." That is predictable. Rock music doesn't cure rebellion; it creates and accelerates it.

I'm not an expert on rock music, so I cannot speak from experience, but I simply don't like its sound and am grieved at the harmful effect it has had on those who submit to its influence, including many of the youngsters who have attended our church or Christian high school. Bob Larsen, however, is an expert on the subject. As a young man, he was a budding recording artist when God called him to preach. Among other things he has specialized in a study of rock for many years. We spoke together at a humanism conference in Little Rock, Arkansas, recently, and I listened intently as he educated 2,400 people on the subject.

The term *rock and roll,* he pointed out, taken from the ghetto community and meaning "fornication," was first applied to the music and gyrations of Elvis Presley back in 1954. That started a musical revolution that integrated aggressive music and aggressive sex. He then noted that rock music is filled with open challenges to sexual activity, ridicules virtue, and exalts "availability." Rock stars who become teenage idols are often sexually indiscriminate, and some are sexual perverts who use their lyrics to advocate their lifestyle. Bob has written an excellent book, published by Tyndale House, entitled *Rock*. I recommend it as essential reading for every parent of teenagers. And after your perusal, pass it along to your son or daughter.

Most Christian parents are extremely naive about rock music, mainly because they cannot understand the words or message. One experience in our Christian high school illustrates my point. In clarifying the anti-moral message of a particular song, a teacher could not recall the words, so one of the students promised to bring them the next day. During the succeeding class that girl began to write the lyrics from memory. The teacher of the class walked up behind her, read them over her shoulder, decided that he had chanced upon a budding young sex pervert who was writing out her bizarre sexual obsession in poetic form, and took her to the principal. When the parents arrived, they didn't believe her story, so they called in the first teacher, who recounted the events of the morning. Everyone was somewhat relieved, but they were not ready for the answer to her mother's question, "Where did you learn such trashy poetry?" The daughter replied, "From the record you bought me last Saturday." That mother could hardly believe that she had innocently spent $8.95 for a sexually indecent gift that could pollute the mind of the child she treasured and dreamed would grow up to be a virtuous young woman.

Many of those who study the subject believe that the sound and beat of rock are capable of destroying the emotions or at least inflaming the fleshly lusts that are so easily ignited in young people. At a time when young people need to be nurtured in the things of the Lord, Satan wants to captivate them with the ways of the world. Among entertainers, there are probably no greater emissaries of Satan than some of the leaders of the rock music field. Bob Larsen verifies that many of them are not only involved with immorality and perversion, but blasphemy, drugs, the occult, and cults.

One of the most incredible stories I have ever heard about rock music was brought to my attention by Steve Beyer, our junior high youth pastor. Being a guitarist himself and, in his pre-Christian days, a rock listener, he is well-acquainted with the subject. He indicated that a recording by a well-known rock group had a secret message to Satan when played backward. The words to the song were harmless enough when the record was played normally, but through electronic means, Steve was able to record the song backwards, and a clear, haunting chant to Satan was unmistakable. As incredible as that sounds, I have heard it.

We must conclude that there is something Satanic about rock music.

A former rock artist performed on the 700 Club, then testified that two years previously he was converted to Christ while the lead guitarist in the band of one of the best-known rock musicians of our day. He confessed that he was heavily into drugs, had participated in unbelievable orgies, and had even engaged in homosexual acts with that same teenage idol. He was now transformed by the power of Christ and had left that filthy business. But the rock star is still polluting the morals and minds of a nation's youth.

Rock music is a vicious enemy of the family and should have no place in a Christian home.

15

Homosexuality

Twenty years ago homosexuality was no real threat to the family—or so we thought. It was considered a sign of mental illness by psychiatrists and was considered illegal by the police; the Kinsey Report suggested that only 4 percent of the population had experienced at least one homosexual contact.

Since then homosexuality has come out of the closet, walked brazenly down the street or corridor of high schools and colleges, and been openly endorsed by prominent movie and TV stars, as well as some feminists. Currently a battle is raging to determine whether or not the straight community will permit homosexuals to teach their school-age children. Two years ago homosexuality claimed 10 percent of the population; now homosexuals want us to believe they total 15 percent!

Naturally it is to their political advantage to inflate their numbers as much as possible. Their growth in our population may have reached 8 percent. TV situation comedy, which has given it an aura of respectability, bears no small responsibility for its recent growth rate.

My book on homosexuality, published three years ago, caused such an avalanche of correspondence that we had to open a Counseling by Mail program just to help homosexuals and their families. Booksellers tell me it strikes far more Christian families than anyone dreamed just a few years ago. Parents are traumatized when they first learn that their child is homosexual, but a wife or husband experiences even greater repugnance when she or he discovers that the partner has embraced that life-style. Many pastors are called into heartbreaking situations that will increase unless society faces the fact that homosexuality is a perversion of our God-given sex drive.

Sex was not designed as an end unto itself. It serves two basic purposes: propagation of the race and a unifying source of pleasure, between a husband and wife, in marriage. Any other use of sexual expression is in violation of God's Word and a perversion of nature. By giving homosexuality social acceptance and respectability, we only make it easier for insecure individuals who may have developed a same-sex tendency to experiment with it and settle into a life-style that produces misery, suffering, and heartache for both homosexuals and their families. After reading hundreds of letters from them, I am even more convinced than when I wrote my book that thousands are unnecessarily swept into homosexuality because of our humanistically inspired leniency toward it.

Often I have wished that homosexual advocates could sit with me in the counseling room and hear a young wife and mother pour out her brokenhearted message of disillusionment, shattered dreams, resentment, and self-rejection because the partner she thought was straight had reverted to the sexual life-style she never knew existed. If you are thinking, *That is no threat to my family,* you are simply echoing the thoughts of those I have counseled. The families of two conservative congressmen felt that way before their tragic stories filled the papers. Homosexuality always happens to someone else— until it hits home.

Compassion and Acceptability

As I have detailed in *What Everyone Should Know About Homosexuality,* many homosexuals are being helped, through Christian counseling and through the power of Jesus Christ, to forsake that life-style. But we will never help them unless we show love to them. As Christians we can never accept that life-style and remain true to the Scriptures. However, we can love them through Christ and seek to help them as He would, if they are willing to repent and use His power to live the new life in Christ. But you will not see lasting fruit or a spiritual reversal until they get victory over their thought lives. As with heterosexuals, victory over sin begins and ends in the mind. Either we control our thoughts, or our thoughts will control us. The Bible teaches that we must be, "Casting down imaginations, and every high thing that exalteth itself against the knowledge of God, and bringing into captivity every thought to the obedience of Christ" (2 Corinthians 10:5).

Why a Threat to the Family

The social pressure caused by some educators, the media, and militant homosexuals has intimidated almost everyone into silence on the subject today. Even the most ardent moral activists are making almost no attempt to reverse the excessively lenient laws and practices that make homosexuality a very real threat to any family. Most morality spokesmen content themselves with opposing further deterioration of our laws, particularly in permitting homosexuals to teach school and, under the guise of academic freedom, to advocate their chosen life-style. The truth is, however, that unless it is culturally branded as wrong, homosexuality will offer a credible option to impressionable young people.

Do not misunderstand, I am not advocating a witch hunt against homosexuals. But if we do not reverse the lenient government policies of the Carter administration, which removed homosexuals from the list of those who are not entitled to immigrate into our country or those who are not eligible for government employment at all levels, they will continue to work their way into positions of influence in our society. They already are far too influential to assure the moral sanity of the next generation. So far few voices are calling for a return to the homosexual policies of 1970. If we do not nullify the trend, that sin will continue to be a threat to the traditional family.

The Christian position in a free culture like ours should be loving compassion and aid for the homosexual, on the one hand, combined with vigorous opposition to any policy that will spread homosexuality. But of one thing you can be certain: Homosexuality in its current form is a definite threat to any family; none is immune. As I travel the country I am frequently confronted with brokenhearted parents who speak of a son or daughter they never dreamed was vulnerable to this sin, now being engulfed by it.

One lad, expelled from a Christian college, met me with his parents and shared the tragic story. He was the only one of a large group—led by a faculty member—caught. Most Christians cannot conceive of the extent of this problem, and all tend to think *It couldn't happen to us.*

If any parent wishes to assist his child in avoiding this tendency, he must start by helping the child to accept his sexuality early in life. Never let a child think you wish he was different from what he is. The key to a normal sex direction is for the individual to be happy with his sexual identity. Girls should be led to appreciate their femininity and womanliness, just as boys should enjoy their masculinity.

16

Ignorance of Family-Life Principles

Nothing is more important in any person's life than his home or family. Unfortunately most of those who marry and set out to raise a family are ignorant of what it takes to construct an effective marriage. The average young man knows more about overhauling the engine of his car than he does about interpersonal relationships,

family finances, child discipline, showing love, or raising children with a reverence toward God.

We spend $140 billion a year on education in our country, offering "pragmatic" courses in such areas as self-actualized psychology, horseback riding, and the occult. Yet many young people graduate from high school functionally illiterate and unprepared for any vocation. Worst of all, they have no formal training in getting along with the most important people in their lives, the members of their own households.

Is it too much to expect of the public school that a twelfth-grade graduate, approximately eighteen years old, know something about the value, use, and budgeting of money? Not a few young people that age do get married early, and about 65 percent of the others will within four years. Yet millions are ignorant of such things as keeping a checkbook, bargain hunting, and the need to avoid credit buying. Why is this a legitimate question in today's society? Because any counselor will tell you that one of the leading causes of marital disharmony is money squabbles—usually the couple is hopelessly in debt.

As we saw in the chapter on materialism, credit buying is a way of life today, but shouldn't someone "educate" our young in the need to deny themselves some of the things they want before they destroy the marriage they need to preserve? Those overly defensive of public school will say, "That isn't the school's responsibility!" My question is, "Why isn't it?" The schools have taken unto themselves the responsibility to entice children and young people to be "sexually active," why not train them how to cope with the responsibilities of such action—like being good parents? They have been taught "self-awareness," "self-discovery," and preparation for world citizenship. Why not the necessities of life? Today's "education," if it can be called that, is incitement to selfishness, the ruin of marriage, and family life.

"How old is a person when he is old enough to get married?" is a question I have been asked many times. Surprisingly, there is no age limit. I have known eighteen-year-olds who were ready, but I also know seventy-year-olds who are not. Maturity is the key, and that means unselfishness.

The one thing that all babies have in common is that they are born selfish. We all need to be trained out of that natural tendency. Our parents get the first crack at teaching us to "grow up," meaning, learning to think of someone else before ourselves. Unfortunately, today the regressive education of John Dewey and his secular-humanist followers has educated a whole generation of high-school and college graduates who are looking for "the good life" through self-actualization, or other academic forms of self-seeking. A value-free diploma is a certificate in ignorance if all it qualifies a person for is business, teaching, or the trades and has not trained him in the most important arena of his life: marriage, family, and parenthood.

Dr. Thomas Holmes of the University of Oregon did a twenty-five year study of the effects of stress on human beings. He and his researchers listed forty-three events in life and gave numerical designations to each according to how much stress they produced on people. The only one they gave 100 points to was "the death of a spouse." After that came: divorce, 73; marital separation, 65; down to marriage, 50. Of the top seven most stress-producing events in life, six had to do with the family.

That study should tell us something: namely that the family is the most important thing in life. As such it deserves priority effort and training to make it successful and meaningful.

Most of the people I have counseled through the years were victims of family ignorance. Many of the over 1 million divorces last year could have been avoided if the couples had known how to safeguard their homes and relationships against the forces working toward the destruction of today's family, as described in this book.

Part of the problem, of course, is to face the fact that problems exist, in the first place. Humanists would not, for they have caused most of them. They don't even consider divorce a problem, but a matter of choice for every free individual. Like everything else, however, Christian teachings are diametrically opposed to those of humanism. Consequently we will find no solutions in secular humanistic thought.

Instead we must turn to the Word of God, which does indeed provide answers to the problems of life. The rest of this book is dedicated to presenting these answers to dispel the ignorance that plagues America today, caused primarily by the humanistic take-over of education, TV, the media, the entertainment field, and even our government.

Interestingly enough, with all the problems plaguing the land, many families still enjoy joyful and meaningful relationships together, either as Christian homes or those committed to traditional moral values. In the church millions of happy families have trained themselves in the Word of God. In fact, we pastors have watched many homes, wracked by the tragedies of the forces of humanism, come to our church, accept Jesus Christ and His Word as their guide and manual of instruction, and discover their homelife literally transformed. The proof of the pudding is in the eating, they tell us. The changes occasioned by Christ's teachings bear evidence that they contain reality.

A couple with two small children, invited to our church by a friend, was in serious trouble! In five years of marriage there was nothing they had not tried. They were the oldest-looking twenty-five-year-olds I had ever seen. Within a month they both received Christ and were immediately channeled into a Bible study. Within a year they were completely transformed. They not only looked better, but seemed younger. Today their treatment of each other is beautiful to watch, and if we rehearsed the kind of lives they lived just fourteen months ago, you wouldn't believe it. The marriage that once hung by a thread is now flourishing, and their house has become a home. Whenever I see their two beautiful little girls, I hesitate to think what they would have become had not their young parents received Christ and started building their family on the principles of God.

17

How to Survive the Battle for the Family

A good-looking young couple, obviously very much in love, thanked me for my lecture in Omaha, Nebraska. "You have given us hope for the future, in spite of the many problems confronting the family today." They explained that several speakers had painted such bleak pictures of the problems faced by contemporary

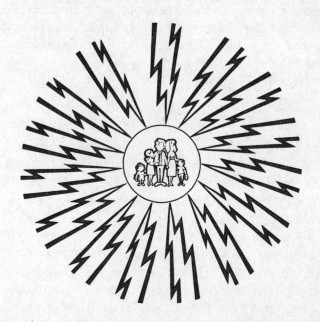

couples that they had almost despaired of getting married or, if they did, of bringing children into our humanism-controlled society. I laughed and reminded them, "Don't forget, it wasn't too swift in the first century, when the early Christians lived under Roman rule. Their leaders were corrupt—in fact, some of their emperors were moral degenerates—yet the homes established by those young believers raised the evangelists that turned that nation completely around in just three centuries."

As the couple walked away hand in hand, I knew I had to write this book. We must offer a message of hope to America! The stranglehold of the humanists on our country is not irreversible. Even if it was, our children would not necessarily become victims of the evils I have portrayed in the previous chapters. We can still reverse the national trend if enough people will wake up to the dangers that the religion of humanism has brought upon us and oppose it with God's help. God has given us resources with which to insulate the Christian home against all evil forces, if we are serious about using them.

The real purpose of this book is not to frighten Christians into celibacy or childless families, but to alert them to the realistic dangers of the enemies that humanism has so cleverly pitted against us. Married couples must concentrate all their spiritual resources in order to preserve the family.

Your Spiritual Resources

The Bible promises us ". . . He who is in you is greater than he that is in the world" (1 John 4:4 NKJV–NT). Our Lord said, ". . . if the strong man knew in what hour the thief would come, he would have watched, and would not have suffered his house to be broken up" (see Matthew 24:43). The problems that confront Christian families today are too serious to take lightly. Just being a Christian is not adequate insulation against today's brand of evil. As long as the humanists remain in power, unsuspecting Christians will continue losing their children to the flesh pots of Washington, D.C.; Hollywood; Dallas; Sin City, U.S.A.; and even your hometown.

Those Christians who seriously use their churches, the Word of God, and the ministry of the Holy Spirit will still be able to raise

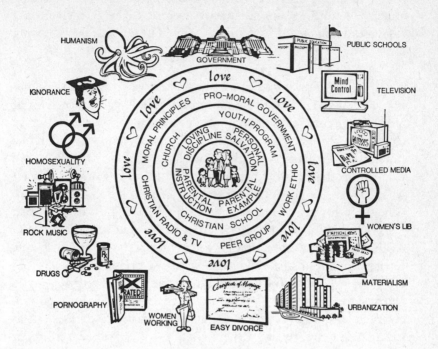

their families to love and serve God. It won't be easy, but historically it never has been. This world system has always been opposed to the will and ways of God. Consequently, raising Christian children has always taken prayer, love, training, and sacrifice. But nothing we do in life is more important, because our children are both our greatest treasure and the future of America. They are well worth the time and effort it takes to insulate them from the forces that would destroy their destiny.

The most powerful ring of insulation against the attacks we have discussed is your spiritual resources. We are taught in the Scriptures that "We wrestle not against flesh and blood, but against . . . spiritual wick

edness in high places" (Ephesians 6:12). To counter these Satanic attacks on our lives and homes, we need to utilize all the spiritual resources available to us. No family should be without the following four.

1. A Personal Salvation Experience for Each Member of the Family God has so planned that every person shall give an account of himself to his heavenly Father, which explains why it is essential for children to have their own conversion experiences. If we, as parents, could invite Christ into our children's hearts, by faith, doubtless we would. But that is an experience the child must gain for himself when he reaches that age at which he understands with his head, believes in his heart, and surrenders his will to the call of Christ.

For most children who are raised in a Christian home and attend a Bible-teaching church, that experience occurs at a very early age. In the case of our first child, who was very responsive to spiritual things, she understood basic biblical truth sufficiently to invite Christ into her heart at four years of age. Now she is married to a minister, and two of her three children have received the Saviour at nearly the same early age. Others of our children waited until six or seven. Parents should be sensitive to the spiritual yearnings of each child. Do not pressure very young children, lest their desire be to please you rather than surrender their own wills to Jesus Christ. On the other hand, older children should be an increasing object of prayerful concern by their parents, if they have not received Christ before their twelfth birthday.

Wise parents will occasionally give opportunity for their young children to rehearse their conversion experiences in order to keep them fresh and personal in their minds, either by reminding them of the details or by helping them to verbalize them. In addition, the Bible says, "Let the redeemed of the Lord say so." Children need to hear occasionally how their parents came to Christ and the events surrounding the conversion of their brothers and sisters.

The individual conversion has been mentioned first because it is the most basic spiritual experience. If parents take this step for granted, the children may enter the precarious stages of puberty and youth without it. Young people frequently turn away from the

Lord, His church, and their parents, when confronted with drugs, rock, and humanism in school, because they lack this foundational spiritual experience to insulate them from temptation.

2. *Spirit-Filled Family Living* The difference between a Christian home and Spirit-filled family living is like day and night. A Christian home is certainly better for everyone involved than an unsaved family, but oftentimes an unseen guest would not be able to tell the difference, except on Sunday. Six days a week they may live just like any other neighbor on the street: active, hectic, and at times even angry and cantankerous. On Sunday they race around, getting ready for the mad dash to Sunday school and church.

Spirit-filled family living is quite different. These parents take seriously the Holy Spirit's commands to "walk in the Spirit ..." (Galatians 5:16) and "Continually be filled [or controlled] with the Spirit" (*see* Ephesians 5:18). Such a home will not always be perfect, but most of the time "love, joy, peace, longsuffering, gentleness, goodness, faith, meekness, and self-control" will form the dominant tone of such a family. Members will still be faced with pressure, testing, and temptation, but they will usually respond in the control of the Spirit, rather than the selfishness, anger, depression, and worry that mark most families.

In two of my other books, *Spirit-Controlled Temperament* (Tyndale) and *Spirit-Controlled Family Living* (Revell), I have already detailed the principles of the Spirit-filled life so I will not do so here. You should, however, know the scriptural results and the six steps for walking in the Spirit, described in chapter 18, "Future of the Family."

The Emotional Results of Walking in the Spirit

1. A song in your heart
2. A thanksgiving attitude
3. A submissive spirit

Speaking to one another in psalms, hymns, and spiritual songs, singing and making melody in your heart to the Lord, giving

thanks always for all things to God the Father in the name of
our Lord Jesus Christ, submitting to one another in the fear of
God.

Ephesians 5:19–21 NKJV–NT

The man has yet to be married who wouldn't enjoy coming home
each day to a wife with a song in her heart, a thanksgiving attitude,
and a submissive spirit. Nor is there a Christian wife who wouldn't
find pleasure in a husband who returned each night with these same
emotional characteristics.

Much of the conflict in the modern family is caused either by
misunderstanding of or by the refusal to accept the role each member was designed by God to fulfill, as clearly defined in the most
important family instruction in the Bible, Ephesians 5:33 through
6:4.

> Wives, submit yourselves to your own husbands, as to the
> Lord. . . . Therefore, just as the church is subject to Christ, so let the
> wives be to their own husbands in everything.
>
> Ephesians 5:22, 24 NKJV–NT

> Husbands, love your wives, just as Christ also loved the church
> and gave himself for it, that He might sanctify and cleanse it with
> the washing of water by the word.
>
> Ephesians 5:25, 26 NKJV–NT

> Children, obey your parents in the Lord, for this is right. "Honor
> your father and mother" which is the first commandment with
> promise: "that it may be well with you and you may live long on the
> earth."
>
> Ephesians 6:1–3 NKJV–NT

> And you fathers, do not provoke your children to wrath, but
> bring them up in the training and admonition of the Lord.
>
> Ephesians 6:4 NKJV–NT

Although these verses are clear and direct in their teaching, many
Christians live as if they were not in the Bible. That is understandable, due to the prevalence of humanistic thinking, which is diametrically opposed to each one of these concepts. Humanism would
have the wife assert her "rights," the husband become either passive
or determined in his quest to "get all the gusto" he can get out

of this "me" generation, and the children be obsessed with their "rights" instead of their responsibilities. Consequently, two successive generations of rebels have sprung forth from American homes.

By contrast, children feel secure in a home where the father acts as the head of the family, lovingly cares for their mother, loves and respects God, and trains them to obey His principles. It is essential to family harmony that the wife submit to her husband's leadership for the Lord's sake. Such a woman will enjoy the love, respect, protection, and provision of her husband; and she will provide her children with an example of the proper role model of a woman, even in today's society.

The Bible addresses only two commands to children: "obey your parents" and "honor your mother and father." Both are in contrast to the philosophy of child advocates and humanist government bureaucrats, who consider parents unqualified to raise their own children, consequently needing the assistance of government-controlled child-care centers, parent effectiveness training, Planned Parenthood, and government-sponsored (and humanist-run) youth centers (sometimes referred to as Youth Health Care Centers). Such measures would only compound the already existing conflicts that humanism has created between parents and their children, and they would hasten the chaos that is inevitable if our country continues in the direction of humanism and strays from the biblical principles upon which America was founded.

Children raised in Spirit-controlled families will be "nurtured" (trained) and "admonished" (instructed) "in the Lord" (the principles of God found in the Bible, which everyone needs in order to live a happy and effective life). Such instruction, given in love, is not harmful, as the humanists would have us believe, but is essential to the successful living of a fulfilled life. The Bible is a "lamp unto our feet" and "a light unto our pathway." Without its principles, no one is equipped to face life, no matter how well educated he is.

The wisest man who ever lived declared, "Hear, ye children, the instruction of a father, and attend to know understanding" (Proverbs 4:1).

Get wisdom, get understanding: forget it not; neither decline from the words of my mouth. Forsake her not, and she shall preserve thee: love her, and she shall keep thee. Wisdom is the principal thing; therefore get wisdom: and with all thy getting get understanding. Exalt her, and she shall promote thee: she shall bring thee to honour, when thou dost embrace her. She shall give to thine head an ornament of grace: a crown of glory shall she deliver to thee. Hear, O my son, and receive my sayings; and the years of thy life shall be many.

Proverbs 4:5–10

3. Consistent Christian Example   Children are the world's greatest imitators. Just as angry and selfish children are reared in angry, selfish homes, so loving, joyful, and thankful children come out of Spirit-filled homes, because they have seen these characteristics exemplified in the conduct of their parents. Integrity, honesty, industry, and consideration for others are not only taught but caught by children as they grow up, if such traits appear on a day-to-day basis in the lives of their parents.

The power of a good example to overcome the harmful forces working to destroy our youth cannot be overestimated. In the youth ministry of our church, from which hundreds of young people have entered the ministry or some form of Christian work as a life vocation, the pastoral staff has noted that such youngsters usually come from two kinds of families: Spirit-filled homes of consistency or families in which one or both parents are not Christians. Young people can understand their parents' unchristian behavior if they are not believers, so it doesn't always have an adverse effect upon them. But they cannot cope with inconsistent carnality from those who should be walking in the Spirit. The greatest blessing any parent can give his child is a consistent example in the home. Its powerful impact can extend even to the third and fourth generation (Exodus 20:5).

4. Loving Discipline   The worst experience for any child is to regularly get his own way. But almost every child tries: Human nature insists on it. That is why he must learn, in the home, to control his desires by self- or parental denial. If he does not receive that loving discipline from his parents, he will grow up to be a self-guided missile waiting for a disaster.

For thirty-five years a form of permissivism that grew out of humanistic psychology has been popular in our country, and as a result three generations of self-indulgent people have become very hostile if they could not assert their wants or "rights." The exception to that general rule of thumb are those who were blessed with parents cognizant of the biblical principle "He that spares the rod hates his son."

As a veteran father I will admit that disciplining my children was the most difficult aspect of fatherhood, but it was essential. In fact, not until my son had to spank his own boy did he really understand that it did hurt me worse than it did him. The necessity of that kind of discipline is not only confirmed in the Bible many times (Proverbs 13:24; Proverbs 23:13; Proverbs 23:14; Proverbs 29:15) but validated in life. Susanna Wesley, the successful mother of seventeen children, said, "The child that does not learn to obey his parents in the home will not obey God or man out of the home." Children need instruction, but they also require correction, particularly when they demonstrate rebellion.

Dr. James Dobson, the child psychologist whose best-selling books on parental instruction are among the finest in print, teaches that parents should carefully distinguish between the mistakes a child makes and the rebellion he expresses. For example, I have heard him say, "Never spank a child for mistakes, but always spank him for rebellion." The Bible teaches, "Rebellion is as the sin of witchcraft."

Two Warnings

All parental discipline should be administered in love, never under the influence of anger. The fire of rage directed at the child becomes part of the problem. Always wait until you have calmed down, then apply the appropriate discipline. If you don't, much of the effectiveness of your training will be lost on the child, who recognizes that your anger is wrong. Somehow your love for the child should be so strong that it manifests itself even when you apply a spanking or require confinement to the home. Always make it a rule, within fifteen minutes of the last tear or at the first expression of repentance, to caress your child warmly. If he is small, spend extra time holding him in your arms.

Second, always be careful, when spanking a child, to do it in a way that is not injurious. God created the bottom not only to sit on but to serve as a well-cushioned seat of learning. Angry parents often discipline much too vigorously. Usually your disapproval and the anticipation of a spanking is enough. After that, only a little pressure in the right spot will convey your message. It is never advisable to strike a child anywhere else, particularly on the face or head.

Parents need to be particularly cautious today when disciplining their children, because some humanists in government spend all their time ferreting out and attacking parents who believe in discipline, accusing them of child abuse. We have met parents who lost custody of their children after spanking them for running away from home or going to school dances; in some cases they had their children taken away because the parents required church attendance. It is a sad commentary on our government that child advocates have worked themselves into such positions that they can use the government to advance their humanist ideas of putting children's rights above parents' rights; that places them 180° in opposition to the key biblical mandate in this area: "Children obey your parents." Until our government is returned to those who pay for it—namely, the majority of taxpayers, who hold traditional moral values—parents would be advised to act cautiously in disciplining their children.

Family-Life University

The home should be the world's greatest university. Mother and father are universally the most important teachers in the life of a child, although they are not always the most effective. God has given parents a special place in the hearts of their children, particularly during their early years, when they can teach them almost anything. Moses must have had this in mind when he said, "And these words, which I command thee this day, shall be in thine heart: And thou shalt teach them diligently unto thy children, and shalt talk of them when thou sittest in thine house, and when thou walkest by the way, and when thou liest down, and when thou risest up" (Deuteronomy 6:6, 7).

Unfortunately most parents have remanded the responsibility for the education of their young to the public school, which is totally unqualified to teach people, because in accord with their humanistic doctrine, they have rejected all responsibility for inculcating moral values and character building (in many cases, as we have seen, they teach against morality and call it values clarification). An education without moral values is very dangerous. In fact atheists without an education are far less dangerous to America than those with graduate degrees, who teach the gifted young people in college and graduate school. If America's 275,000 humanists, who control our 3,000 secular (public) colleges and universities, the TV networks, newspapers, magazines, government bureaucracies, judgeships, radical liberal organizations, unions, local school boards, and other agencies of major influence, were removed from their positions for just four years, so that our 63 million young people were subjected to basic traditional moral values, character building, and self-discipline in the midst of their educational process, 90 percent of the social problems in this country would fade away.

Since the likelihood of that happening for a few years is slim, we had better look for another way of solving the problem. The solution to the education question is to send children to a Christian school, if possible, and for parents to return to the biblical mandate requiring them to use the home in teaching their own children the ways of God. Because young children have extremely curious and impressionable minds, they should be exposed to biblical truth early and regularly by the two most effective teachers in their lives: mom and dad. Such instruction will provide excellent insulation against humanism's battle for their minds. The following four teaching methods will provide an excellent curriculum for your family college:

1. Daily family devotions: Most Bible-teaching churches encourage their families to spend ten to thirty minutes a day in family worship or daily devotions. This simple but effective family habit provides many benefits. It not only trains the children to acknowledge and respect God, but creates in them an early responsiveness to His Word as a book above all others, which is valuable to read daily. The father should lead in this short devotional time, establishing it as an important priority throughout life, particularly when the children are in their teen years.

Daily devotions provide an opportunity for parents to teach their children to pray and to discuss principles from the Bible. Your Bible bookstore contains several good books and aids on this subject, if your church does not supply such materials. The following sample outline may prove helpful:

1. Read the Bible—one chapter or less if the children are small.
2. Read the daily-devotional guide.
3. Briefly discuss what you have read—ask the children simple questions on the subject.
4. Review a Scripture memory verse.
5. Assign subjects for prayer.
6. Assign prayer requests.
7. Pray—one or two children, depending on size of family, and one parent, each day.
8. Sing a happy song or chorus everyone knows.

2. Bible storybooks: A sage once warned, "You are what you read." I believe that reading is the most powerful educational tool available. In fact, if you can read, you can learn almost anything. In my childhood I developed a voracious appetite for reading, which has never been checked. Such an appetite can be cultivated in small children by providing them with some of the incredibly interesting reading materials that are available in Christian bookstores. All children should be surrounded by good, colorful, and interesting Bible stories; books about the Bible; or wholesome fiction based on biblical principles. Don't underestimate the power of clean fiction to whet a child's appetite for learning. The devil and his humanist publishers know that well. As I walk through airport bookshops,

I note that best-selling books flood the racks, most of them fiction. Some parents feel obliged to narrow their child's reading to the Bible, but that is too unrealistic. As a young man, I devoured everything Zane Grey wrote, and believe it or not, fed upon an entire lifetime of Frank Merriwell magazines that a man had saved in his basement for forty years. Actually, I got burned out on fiction and haven't read a complete novel since I was college age, but I have made it a policy to read thirty books a year, since then. Every parent should foster a thirst for reading in his child and then provide wholesome, uplifting books. Almost nothing sold in the secular marketplace is fit for human consumption, because of its anti-moral teachings. That is why you should carefully select your child's reading from a Christian bookstore. Knowing that I was going to recommend good Christian reading as a means of insulating your family's mind from the evil attacks of humanism, I wrote to several Christian publishers for samples of their best children's literature. To my amazement I received three boxes full of such materials, much of which is superb.

I would hasten to add that some excellent Bible-story cassettes are available in Bible bookstores today. I have watched my grandchildren sit enthralled by the colorful sounds of God's wonderful Word. There are also recordings of good music, Bible studies, and Scripture readings that make wonderful gifts for family listening.

Speaking of cassette listening, one of the most effective features of our ministry to families is our Family Life Cassette of the Month Club (COM, as we call it). We produce the finest biblically based materials available in the country today, featuring twenty-two of the best family-life teachers, lecturers, and speakers in the country (those who are interested should write to Family Life COM Club, Box 1299, El Cajon, CA 92022, for a free brochure and catalog). Home video recordings may well be the next educational tool we can bring into our homes for family survival.

3. Bible study: During the evening, when the family is home together, do a Bible study with the children. Two or three nights can sometimes be spent on Sunday-school lessons. Play Bible games together or have a thirty-minute quiet time, as does one family I know, when each one pursues his own Bible study. In our church, as many as 1,500 people read the Bible through each year, at the rate of approximately four chapters daily.

4. *Memorization of Scripture:* This is one of the best safeguards I know of against sin. Many Scriptures administer the challenge to "keep your heart diligently." The path to your heart leads through the mind. If you would keep the hearts of your children from this world system's humanistic attacks, you will first have to keep their minds. How? Fill their minds with the Word of God. Memorization is strenuous work, but it pays tremendous dividends. In my book *How to Study the Bible for Yourself,* I have a list of over 150 key verses to memorize. You can purchase Scripture-memorization cards in your Bible bookstore, from the Navigators, or from Family Life Seminars (Box 1299, El Cajon, CA 92022). You can even make up your own.

As my wife and I look back on the raising of our children, the one program on which we would spend more time would be Scripture memorization. We did some, but if I had known then what I know now, I would have disregarded the theories of the educators that "rote learning was not educationally sound" or "one shouldn't teach children to memorize things they do not understand." That is nonsense! Obviously they will profit nothing from what they have not learned.

When I was a junior-high and high-school boy, our family was so poor that we couldn't afford the money for me to attend church camp. Fortunately our Sunday school and Vacation Bible School conducted an annual Scripture memory contest, offering free passage to camp for the winner and half-fare for the runner-up. When I heard that, I made up my mind to be the winner each year. An older boy in our church, named Frank, was the competition, and for five years one of us garnered first or second place, both of us going to camp for either full or half price. For years as a pastor-teacher of the Word, I have clipped the dividends from that Bible memorization, both in my preaching and in my writing. In addition, principles early committed to memory have helped me to understand the evils of humanism.

While holding a seminar in Grand Rapids, I recognized a man

who came to greet me after the Friday-night session as my boyhood friend Frank. To my question, "Where have you been all these years?" he replied, "I've been a missionary to South America for twenty-seven years." As our plane flew out of Grand Rapids the next day, I couldn't help thinking that, between us, we have given sixty years of service to Jesus Christ and raised nine children, several of whom have gone into church work. Now you can understand why I am convinced that Scripture memorization for children and young people is an excellent way to insulate their minds "against the wiles of the devil," which, today, is atheistic humanism in its multiple forms.

Four Family Resources

In addition to these teaching methods you can use in your family, there are four resources outside the family that can help you to grow and become strong in the things of the Lord.

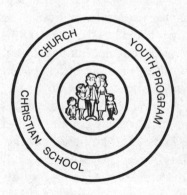

The Church as a Resource The greatest friend of the family is the church, and that is as our Creator intended. When I say *church,* I am assuming a Bible-teaching church that communicates God's principles for family living to its members. We have already determined that public education, which seems obsessed with a desire to teach sex education without benefit of moral values, is almost bankrupt as a positive influence on family life. So obsessed with self-satisfaction and autonomy are the humanist curriculum planners and textbook writers that they fail to teach self-denial and the other self-control ingredients necessary to maintain lasting interpersonal relationships. Only in the church do we hear teaching on unselfishness, love, sharing, giving, trust, truth, and faithfulness, all essential ingredients of happy family living. In addition, we learn how to avoid jealousy, anger, bitterness, and other destroyers of human relationships. Government cannot aid us with these subjects, for it has transferred family education to the schools, which act as a turncoat to the family—except for those dedicated traditional moralists still in public education, who use their platform to communicate true values. Many humanist administrations make life miserable for such educators, assuming that academic freedom does not include the right to teach morals or values. TV and the media cannot serve family interests, for they are so destructive that they have become archenemies of family life.

That leaves the church as the last true friend upon whom the family can depend. The Gallup Poll estimates that over 100 million adults in America are church members. Except for those who attend liberal churches, which are heavily influenced by humanist teaching (many are members of the National Council of Churches of Christ), church families are exposed to very positive family-life teachings. For example, during the past ten years I have conducted over 375 two-day family seminars, sponsored by the churches of almost every metropolitan area of the nation. In addition I can name several others who have done the same. Currently, hundreds of churches have shown either the family life films of Dr. James Dobson or the set of four films by my wife and me. Sunday-school classes, Bible studies, and evening church services are often utilized for such film showings or for special speakers. In addition every Bible conference in the nation runs weekend couples' conferences that major in family-life teachings. As I travel the country, I find that the Roman Catholic Church has conducted thousands of Marriage Encounters, and the Seventh-Day Adventists, Mormons, and Jews all sponsor training programs and provide a vast supply of literature aimed at improving family life. It is very common for families in trouble to seek help first at the church, further evidence that the church is the family's best friend. Perhaps that is why humanism considers the church its number-one enemy. Humanism is antifamily, while the church is profamily; and if you haven't noticed, that is the burning social battle of our day: humanism, on the one hand, bringing America's families to Sodom and Gomorrah; and the church, on the other, seeking to pull America toward traditional moral values. We hope through this book to awaken thousands of profamily people to the battle: people who will utilize the church to help protect their family and join with us in our fight to wrest control of our society from humanism in its many forms and powerful agencies.

The church in America has undergone an enormous movement of the Spirit of God, as I indicated in my previous book on humanism. In my opinion, that numerical church growth—which Gallup estimates at 60 million born-again adults—is probably the primary factor that has slowed down the humanist juggernaut. The church and her relentless teaching of moral values has opened the eyes of the millions of profamily, pro-life, pro-moral, profreedom, and pro-American patriots, halting the seventy-year pattern of electing and reelecting a majority of anti-moral politicians to make our nation's laws and set her policies.

Sunday School or Sunday Bible Fellowship   As churches grow in numbers, it becomes increasingly difficult to maintain a close fellowship with the people. The weekly Bible study, usually on Sunday morning, provides such an opportunity. These classes, which run from ten to a few hundred, are more informal than church services. They are an able supplement, not a substitute, for the worship service of your church. It is very important that your teens attend Sunday school in order to make friends with their peers, young people whose parents wish their children to grow up with some religious and moral values.

Youth Group   The youth activities in your church can provide a powerful bit of insulation against the attacks of the enemy. In recent years many churches have hired youth pastors, specialists in organizing spiritual, social, educational, and outreach programs that will challenge active young people who need something to occupy their time and energies. Congregations with such programs require sacrifice on your part, but it pays great dividends. In churches that cannot afford a pastor, a dedicated layman often performs that necessary task. If your church has none, why not volunteer your services to the pastor? I'm confident he will welcome your help. We have found that parents of teens often make the best workers; they have a vested interest in the program.

Christian School The Christian school may not be the final solution to the educational problems of our country, but it is definitely the answer to your children's needs today. When our church founded the first Christian high school in San Diego, back in 1965, there were 50 million public-school students and less than 500,000 students in Christian schools. Today Christian schools total almost 5.5 million, while the public schools have dropped to 43 million. That suggests one major change: Parents are dissatisfied with public-school influence on their children. Since parents are already taxpayers, they pay for public education, yet millions are willing to add thousands of educational dollars annually to their budgets, to keep their children from being brainwashed by humanism. Be sure of this: Public education is not free! Today it will probably cost the most valuable asset in your family: your children's minds.

Four of my children have attended our Christian high school, which today is one of the largest in the nation. We also have started a Christian school system so other young people can enjoy our vision for preserving the minds of our nation's youth. If you have a Christian school in your community, I would recommend it for your children, particularly for junior high and senior high, though at the rate humanists are bringing explicit sex education down to the first grade level, it is usually essential for all ages.[1]

Many parents pay tuition they really cannot afford to protect the minds of their children. I pray that after reading this book, you will realize the necessity of a Christian education. One mother in our church testified, at our Mother's Day service, about her excitement that all four of her children were attending our Christian school, even though it cost one-third of their total income. She said, "We never eat out; I make all our clothes; and I have not purchased a new dress in four years, but it is worth every penny when I see what is happening in the lives of my children."

Societal Change

Many Christians share the theological misconception that *societal change* (a term liberal humanists love) is a necessary result of the Last Days. Consequently they have sat on their hands and let this humanist-manipulated societal change continue downward, bringing us ever closer to Sodom and Gomorrah. That has given the humanist minority in our country virtual control over the majority of our population. It is time all pro-moral Americans recognize that we are at war with the anti-moral forces of humanism.

November 4, 1980 was the most exciting election in my lifetime because it convinced me that we pro-family, pro-moral, pro-God types *do* represent the moral yearnings of the American people and that they will follow if we will only lead. I realize that the TV, media, and newspapers still make us sound like a dangerous threat to the nation, but the only danger we offer is to their virtual mastery over the media, which to them is essential in order to maintain control over the great pro-moral majority. Usually the humanists accuse us of the very thing they have perpetrated for years.

The next two off-year presidential elections will determine the fate of America. If in 1982 we can elect a few more senators and congressmen who are committed to morality, and in 1984 and 1988 we elect even more, including presidential candidates who will appoint only pro-moralists to office, this country will move into the 90s in much better shape than it entered the 80s. Can you imagine a federal government so morally committed that we do not have to write or call during times of pending legislation, because we know that our representatives will automatically vote correctly on moral issues?

What are the key moral issues?

1. A human-life amendment to stop the murder of the unborn.
2. A voluntary prayer amendment to allow our children to acknowledge God.
3. A decency-in-literature amendment to make it illegal to sell books and magazines that flaunt, advertise, and encourage acts that are illegal.
4. Stricter law enforcement, particularly for acts of violence and for repeat offenders.
5. Stricter enforcement regarding illegal drugs.
6. Elimination of explicit, value-free sex education in the public schools or on TV.
7. Parents' rights—recognition that children belong to parents, not to government.
8. Recognition that homosexuality is not a normal life-style and should not be advocated in public schools.
9. Acknowledgment that humanism needs to be recognized as a religion and expelled from all public, tax-supported schools.

Government Is Your Business

Your tax dollars pay the salaries of our government officials, therefore you have a vested interest in how they run our country. Traditionally legislators, judges, and politicians were referred to as *public servants.* As such they were responsive to the people who elected them. Gradually that attitude has changed to one of elitism. That is, "The people are too dumb to know what is good for them; therefore we need an elite that makes their laws, sets their policies, and determines their future." This attitude accounts for many governmental decisions contrary to the wishes of the American people: from giving away the Panama Canal to rejecting capital punishment for capital offenses, which is currently favored by 67 percent of the population. This elitist attitude was reflected by a defeated senator when he told me, "I am going to vote my convictions, no matter what my constituents say." Since he voted the humanist line most of the time, he was rightly voted out of office by his nonhumanistic constituency.

The most consistent mistake regarding government that Christian parents have made during the past one hundred years is neglect of the electoral process. Too few Christians have worked for the election of pro-moral candidates, and until 1980, millions did not even register to vote. Thanks to the Moral Majority, Concerned Women for America, the Religious Roundtable, and many other patriotic organizations, 6 to 10 million new voters registered and (based on the outcome) voted on election day. That is good citizenship that helps to insulate the home.

Christians have also mistakenly failed to challenge their young to run for public office or serve in the government. Consequently the positions that should be filled by strong Christians or pro-moralists are assumed by those who do not share our moral values. Since Gallup reports that 20 percent of the population is born again, one out of five politicians and government workers should be born again. Gallup also indicates that an additional 64 percent of the population "believe the Ten Commandments are still valid today." Consequently, 84 out of every 100 government workers or politicians should share traditional moral values, with only 16 percent being of the humanist persuasion. Tragically our age acts as if 16 percent possess traditional moral commitment and 84 percent maintain humanist values. Now do you understand why I keep repeating that until 1980, the minority has been leading the majority? That needs to be changed permanently to bring America back to the traditional moral values upon which it was founded.

The Bible and Civil Government

The Bible is not silent on the subject of civil government. Its teachings, however, have been largely ignored, to the peril of our nation's moral sanity. Consider the following teaching from Romans 13:1-10 (NKJV–NT).

1 Let every soul be subject to the governing authorities. For there is no authority except from God, and the authorities that exist are appointed by God.

2 Therefore whoever resists the authority resists the ordinance of God, and those who resist will bring judgment on themselves.

3 For rulers are not a terror to good works, but to evil. Do you then want to be unafraid of the authority? Do what is good, and you will have praise from the same.

4 For *he is God's minister* to you for good. But if you do what is evil, be afraid; for he does not bear the sword in vain; for he is *God's minister,* an avenger to execute wrath on him who does evil.

5 Therefore you must be subject, not only because of wrath but also for conscience' sake.

6 For because of this you also pay taxes, for they are *God's ministers* attending continually to this very thing.

7 Render therefore to all their due: taxes to whom taxes are due, customs to whom customs, fear to whom fear, honor to whom honor.

Love Your Neighbor

8 Owe no one anything but to love one another, for he who loves another has fulfilled the law;

Christians must obey the law.

Governors, presidents, legislators, authorities are ministers of God, for our good. They should be obeyed.

God's New Testament civil-law code

1. Love your fellowman.
2. Do not commit adultery.
3. Do not murder.

9 and for this, *"You shall not commit adultery," "You shall not murder," "You shall not steal," "You shall not bear false witness," "You shall not covet";* and if there is any other commandment, it is summed up in this saying, namely, *"You shall love your neighbor as yourself."*

10 Love does no harm to a neighbor; therefore love is the fulfillment of the law.

4. Do not steal.
5. Do not bear false witness. (In other words, tell the truth.)
6. Do not covet.

Government is not inherently evil; actually it was instituted by God. But government is only as good as the people who comprise it. Therefore if anti-moral humanists control the government, it will do that which, by traditional moral standards, is evil. As we have seen in chapter five, this evil is often directed at the family. Ironically, the institution God established to protect the family then became the institution to destroy it. Consequently we do not have to disband or overthrow government, that would be illegal. Instead we should work vigorously to remove the antifamily humanists from office, whether from the United States Senate, House of Representatives, or our local school board. By replacing them, through the ballot box, with committed moralists, we can again enjoy peace in our land and a government committed to protecting the family, not destroying it.

The Purpose of Government

SCRIPTURE

Therefore I exhort first of all that supplications, prayers, intercessions, and giving of thanks be made for all men, for kings and all who are in authority, that we may lead a quiet and

MEANING

Government leaders should be the subject of prayer because their purpose is to provide their citizens:

1. Quiet and peaceable lives (free of violence).

peaceable life in all godliness and reverence. For this is good and acceptable in the sight of God our Savior.

   1 Timothy 2:1–3 NKJV–NT

2. Godliness—civil morality.
3. Honesty—enforcement of the law.

Such a government is "good and acceptable in the sight of God our Savior" and profitable for its citizens. Is it not interesting that the very next verse says, "Who desires all men to be saved and to come to the knowledge of the truth," indicating that it is not the government's job to preach the Gospel, but ours as committed Christians. Government must provide a peaceful environment, free of governmental interference, so that Christians living in that country can preach the Gospel, telling all men it is God's will they be saved.

I hope you realize that one of the long-range objectives of humanism is to control our country so that such freedom would be seriously restricted. For example European governments are far more controlled by humanism than ours. That explains why not one Christian-owned radio or TV station exists in Europe or Canada. America has over 350 Christian-owned radio and TV stations, free to preach the Gospel. No wonder the mighty soul harvest of the 70s in America is not shared by Europe. Someone planned it that way—the humanists—and the one they are working for, whom I will identify in my fourth book in this series.

Moral Activism

The kind of change in the governmental leadership of our country that we have been talking about will not just happen. We must make it happen by prayerfully getting involved in the electoral process and by opposing all further deterioration of our legal moral standards. This form of moral activism, disdained by some believers, has already been adapted by millions of Christians. That is why we have been able to slow down the humanist hurricane and have forced them to revise their timetable for complete mind control of America. To our advantage, humanists in government still do not realize how offensive their anti-moral theories are. For example, the California Supreme Court voted five to four that a fourteen-year-old girl could not get an abortion without notifying her parents. However, that does not mean she must have their consent! In other words, parental approval must be sought by a girl to get her ears pierced, but not to seek an abortion! A TV reporter interviewed a government bureaucrat who was obviously displeased with this decision, for she protested, "This ruling will not stop teenage abortions, but it will slow the *emancipation of our children.*"

From whom are the humanist bureaucrats trying to emancipate our children? Why, their parents, of course! Did you not realize your children are slaves—particularly if you forbid them to read pornography, engage in premarital sex, and so on? Such TV comments only serve to catapult more Christians from the moral-passivity fringe of noninvolvement into the center of the action, where they can help turn this country around.

This story from the *Moral Majority Report* is further evidence that government is not *for* the family.

HAVERHILL, Mass.—A few months ago my 15-year-old sister Cathi returned home from school with a wide smirk on her face. She quickly remarked to my mother something about leaving home if anyone tried to make her attend church on Sunday.

This unusually hot desire to rebel followed a paper Cathi had been given in one of her classes. The paper was a listing of several runaway shelters and emergency phone numbers. Passing the list to my mother, Cathi blurted that she would no longer put up with any "unreasonable" requests or rules made by mere parents.

This kind of attitude that parents are promoters of unimportant, outdated morals and values seems to be well nurtured in many high schools today. A certain school guidance counselor recently termed my mother a religious fanatic because she encourages her daughter to be a churchgoer.

He then emphatically stated that he wouldn't recommend religion to any student seeking help.

Many times students look to premarital sex and a host of drugs to fill the gaps in their life because of the liberal attitudes borrowed from their teachers. It is then that parents become enemies in the eyes of the children who once loved and honored them so much.

My sister Cathi is now much more of an expert in the field of sexuality than I am or probably ever will be. Every part of the male and female body and every method of birth control and abortion were discussed openly in her co-ed, sex-ed class. Condoms and birth control pills were passed around for everyone to touch, just so the students could become "familiar" with the different devices. The only thing missing was a visual demonstration of lovemaking positions atop of the teacher's desk. After all of this open discussion my sister probably felt much more self assured about engaging in "sex without fear."

The examples are endless. I didn't even mention the profanity and smutty pornography in some of Cathi's textbooks. The guilty school systems know who they are. They need to stop viewing parents as inconvenient snags standing in the way of student rights.

Parents ought to be able to send a son or daughter to school knowing that the training they received at home won't be constantly refuted and trampled upon by liberals, gays, communists or anyone else. God ordained parents to "train up a child in the way he should go." Teachers and administrators should be a complementary part of the entire process, not organizers of wrongdoing and rebellion.

I thank God for those good teachers who continually reflect sound examples of right living to their students. At the same time I know God's judgement awaits those contributing to the moral decay of my country.

Cathi doesn't live at home anymore. She ran away a day before her 16th birthday. The loving concern and care Cathi received from her parents mean nothing to her.[2]

This is only one of many stories that come to our office, reporting tales of woe that demonstrate the extent to which humanism is destroying a large part of this generation of young people. How well I remember the historians' comments about various wars that destroyed the flower of France or Germany, meaning their young men and future fathers. Humanism is destroying the flower of America's youth through drugs, sex, and antifamily teachings. Millions refuse to give up without a fight.

What Can You Do?

1. Pray for America, as the Scriptures teach (1 Timothy 2:1, 1 Chronicles 7:14). Throughout the country, many groups are calling for prayer, asking that God bring us a national revival. Prayer

vigils and groups have sprung up around the nation. Concerned Women for America has launched a nationwide campaign to establish 50,000 prayer chapters, one in every state, city, and village. Each chapter will have from 7 to 350 members—links in a massive chain that could well bind up the moral ills of the land. (Anyone interested may write Concerned Women for America, P.O. Box 20376, El Cajon, CA 92021.)

2. Form a *MAC* group in your church: that is, a Moral Activity Committee, individuals who will become informed on local, state, and national moral issues and extend their information to the entire church. Disseminating information is the first step toward having an informed group, church, or nation.

3. As a private citizen, work for candidates who share your moral values. In our county three conservative, pro-moral congressmen were elected because a group of Christians worked diligently for their election. One man was converted during the election due to the many Christians who toiled tirelessly in his campaign. Because a team of over three hundred people from five different churches passed out three pieces of literature, one on each of the last three days before the election, he defeated an eighteen-year liberal incumbent by four thousand votes.

4. Circulate voter reports on moral issues. Many of the new pro-family organizations prepare voter indexes on such issues. Take these to your local printer and reproduce them; acquaint your friends with the positions of candidates in your area. This is a tool conservatives can use that very few liberals can imitate, because we are the ones so deeply concerned about the moral direction in which our country is going. They are happy with the status quo.

5. Recruit or help strong pro-moralists run for the school board. If no one else will do it, consider running yourself.

6. Write to your local, state, and national officials whenever they are considering moral issues. They need to hear from you. Be sure to participate as you are able in such programs as "Clean Up TV," "Pass the Human Life Amendment," or anything else that will bring back moral standards in our land.

Protect Your Children

The minds of your children are their most important assets. If TV and radio have taught us anything, it should be that they are unfit for our children. Don't expect your child to be mature enough to monitor his TV viewing, particularly in light of a recent report that the average child in America watches seven hours of TV each day. There isn't that much TV worth watching anymore (except New Year's Day, when one can see four football games).

Instead cultivate your child's taste for books, Christian radio, and selected news, or Christian TV programming. Fifty-seven Christian TV shows are produced weekly (there will soon be one more, Lord willing, for Bev and I soon plan to produce a thirty-minute weekly family program for the family hour). Don't just forbid your children to watch the bad; offer a meaningful alternative. And do it together. The time you spend as a family is a powerful bond that will firmly insulate your children from evil.

Watch Their Peer Groups

"Evil companions corrupt good morals" (see 1 Corinthians 15:33), the verse of Scripture which God revealed in a special way to my widowed mother, kept me from destroying myself when I was seventeen. Recognizing that my boyhood friends of many years did not share my moral values, she gave me the choice of leaving home or breaking off from my friends. In those days I couldn't run off to a youth care center, humanistic guidance counselor, or child advocate who thought humanist bureaucrats knew more about child raising than parents. After learning that no one loved me more than my mother, I returned home and discovered that those kids at the church weren't so bad after all.

I have said this in print before, but it is worth repeating. One of the biggest mistakes Christian parents make is to let their teenagers select their own friends. We are all influenced by our friends—for good or for bad, depending on the friend. And teenage peer pressure is probably the greatest pressure they will ever face. That is why if jeans are "in," they all wear jeans. The same is true of long hair, T-shirts, and so on. If "everyone is doing it," your kids may be persuaded by teen peer pressure to do that which is contrary to your moral values. That is why your young person needs an active church group in which to fellowship—or, if possible, a Christian school.

Young people are most inclined to be emotionally combustible between the ages of fourteen and twenty-four. Therefore screen your offspring from the wrong kind of influence during those very impressionable years.

Survival Through Love

One of the strongest insulations against the external attacks on the family is love. Everyone needs love, particularly teenagers. Admittedly a case can be made for the infant's craving for love, and we

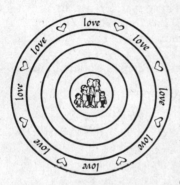

shouldn't omit the toddler, primary, or junior. But the most difficult time to love your kids is when they don't love themselves.

It has never been easy to be a teenager. Between modern technology and the humanist opposition to moral values, it is more difficult than ever before. The insecurity produced in a teenager's mind by conflicting philosophies—situation ethics and permissiveness taught in school, against moral values advocated by parents at home—coupled with the new drives and emotions that course within him, make him very unsure of himself, his values, and his future. Teens who face these pressures supported by love usually make it. Even when they turn their backs on home and family, they usually find that no one else will love them the way their parents and brothers and sisters do.

The Bible says, "Love covers a multitude of sins." Parents can make a number of mistakes raising children (there are no perfect parents—we're too human for that) and still have them turn out right. But that love must be translated into time: quality time in doing things, going places together, and playing together. To this day our children love to play competitive games. (And thanks to the new electronic games, a good use for TV has finally been found.)

As I look back on my childhood, I realize today how rich I was. We never had a rug on the floor, and for many years we didn't own a car. My widowed mother worked nine hours a day, six days a week, and all three of us found jobs before the law allowed. But we were rich! Looking back on that single-parent, church-going family in Detroit, I have the luxury of knowing I was loved. In fact I have the priceless heritage of looking back on my childhood and never remembering a time when I was not loved by the most important person in my life. She loved all three of us enough for two parents.

I could wish for all America's children that kind of love!

Notes

1. If you do not know of a Christian school in your area, write to: Association of Christian Schools, International, P.O. Box 4097, Whittier, CA 90607 or Accelerated Christian Education, P.O. Box 2205, Garland, Texas 75041.
2. Bonnie Jean Silva, "How Parents Become Enemies of Children," *Moral Majority Report,* 2 (16 March 1981), p. 17.

18

The Future of the Family

In 1949 a dying man named George Orwell published a spine-chilling novel depicting a nightmarish totalitarian state. In his book *1984,* every citizen was controlled by "Big Brother" (government)

who, with "Newspeak" (TV nightly news), attempted to control everything in society from family life to the very thoughts of the citizens. Orwell, we must remember, was a committed Marxist as a youth, even to sharing in the unsuccessful Communist attempt to overthrow the Spanish government, during the 30s. The 1948 Russian brutality in stamping out the Hungarian Freedom Fighters awakened him to Communism's totalitarianism. Aware that he was dying of tuberculosis, he wanted to write a novel that would open the eyes of the free peoples of the western world to the fact that socialism was a gradual concentration of power into the hands of the elite few, who wanted to make all the decisions for everyone.

As incredible as it may seem, most of the predictions by Orwell in *1984* have come true. Dr. David Goodman, a psychologist and futurist, made a study of the book and verified that of the 137 prophecies found there, over 100 have come to pass. Perhaps the 1980 rejection of former President Jimmy Carter's liberal humanist government by the American people was in part a fear that four more years of his socialist policies would make *1984*, with all of its overtones of stifling control over individuals and families, a reality. Certainly we were alarmed by the overconfident and unconcealed plans of many of his appointed bureaucrats, calling for such features as "government sponsored [and controlled] day care centers" and "compulsory sex education courses." Some of the bizarre suggestions of the 1980 White House Conference on Families made it easy for many of us to warn voters that the broad road of government was desperately in need of repair.

Hopefully, the conservative Reagan administration will return more individual freedom to families, parents, and local communities, as was the case historically before humanism's socialistic theories became government policy. Many knowledgeable people believe that Americans are beginning to recognize that government cannot give us anything without first taking something away; that our freedoms grow smaller as government grows bigger; and that family members, rather than government, must take care of the institution known as the family. The 1980 landslide election of conservatives has promise of moving *1984* to 1988 or 1992 and quite possibly eliminating it altogether. Whether this turn toward conservatism will be permanent cannot really be known until the next presidential election. I am convinced, however, that the future of family life has been enhanced by the nation's recent conservative choices.

What does the future hold for the family? The answer you receive depends largely on whom you ask. Many of the "change agents" (liberal humanist school teachers) or "social planners" (liberal government bureaucrats who intend to socialize America) or humanist writers will render a much different answer than those who hold traditional American Judeo-Christian moral values. Consider what the popular writer Alvin Toffler—who admitted that in his early life he was a Marxist—has to offer.

> The family has been called the "giant shock absorber" of society—the place to which the bruised and battered individual returns after doing battle with the world, the one stable point in an increasingly flux-filled environment. As the super-industrial revolution unfolds, this "shock absorber" will come in for some shocks of its own.
>
> Social critics have a field day speculating about the family. The family is "near the point of complete extinction," says Ferdinand Lundberg, author of *The Coming World Transformation.* "The family is dead except for the first year or two of child raising," according to psychoanalyst William Wolf. "This will be its only function." Pessimists tell us the family is racing toward oblivion—but seldom tell us what will take its place.
>
> Family optimists, in contrast, contend that the family, having existed all this time, will continue to exist. Some go as far as to argue that the family is in for a Golden Age. As leisure spreads, they theorize, families will spend more time together and will derive great satisfaction from joint activity. "The family that plays together, stays together," etc.
>
> A more sophisticated view holds that the very turbulence of tomorrow will drive people deeper into their families. "People will marry for stable structure," says Dr. Irwin M. Greenberg, Professor of Psychiatry at the Albert Einstein College of Medicine. According to this view, the family serves as one's "portable roots," anchoring one against the storm of change. In short, the more transient and novel the environment, the more important the family will become.
>
> It may be that both sides in this debate are wrong. For the future is more open than it might appear. The family may neither vanish nor enter upon a new Golden Age. It may—and this is far more likely—break up, shatter, only to come together again in weird and novel ways.[1]

The Bible: The Future of the Family

What does the Bible say about the future? Here we encounter good news. It isn't going to pass away! Jesus Christ provided several prophecies about His Second Coming, which He called the Day of the Son of Man. In Luke 17 He predicted what earthly life would be like when He comes again. Read it and note the family conditions that will prevail.

> And as it was in the days of Noah, so it will be also in the days of the Son of Man: They ate, they drank, they married wives, they were given in marriage, until the day that Noah entered the ark, and the flood came and destroyed them all. Likewise also as it was in the days of Lot: They ate, they drank, they bought, they sold, they planted, they built; but the same day that Lot went out of Sodom it rained fire and brimstone from heaven and destroyed them all. Even so will it be in the day when the Son of Man is revealed. In that day, he who is on the housetop, and his goods in the house, let him not come down to take them away. And he who is in the field, likewise let him not turn back. Remember Lot's wife.
>
> Luke 17:26–32 NKJV–NT

No, family life will not become obsolete! Nor will it be replaced, for when our Lord comes, the people will be marrying, giving in marriage, eating, drinking, buying, selling, planting, reaping, working, and living in houses. That sounds like everyday conventional practices that hark back to the beginning of human civilization. Perhaps it will dawn on our humanist social scientists that the family has always been an indispensable part of civilization; without it there would be no society, cultural propagation, or future—even for them.

Conditions, not the family, will change. Families have always adjusted to change, from the farm, to the Industrial Revolution, to the nuclear age—even into the twenty-first century. Like a boat tossed about on the waves, the family has been battered, abused and at times seriously damaged, but it still floats. I think the family will get even stronger, particularly if parents come to recognize the dangerous attacks on the family described in this book, and if they will follow the procedures we have offered for insulating their families from these devilish attacks.

The Electronic Cottage

One interesting prediction by Toffler in his new book, *The Third Wave,* should have a healthy impact on family life. He calls it *The Electronic Cottage.* In the "good old days"—that is, before industry, electricity, cities, and rapid means of travel (which covers over 95 percent of human history)—the home was the center of everything in a person's life. Almost everyone worked out of his home, and family members participated in that work. Farmers raised large families, partly to help with the chores. The housewife did more than household duties; she cut wood, milked cows, fed animals, and so on. The milkman, bread man and small businessman usually operated out of his home. Even the doctor set out his shingle in front of his house.

The Industrial Revolution changed much of that, particularly in the West. For the past 300 years technology has led to specialization, which has had a fragmenting effect on the family. Fathers, during this period, leave for work early and return late. No longer can the average worker take his son to work with him. Today's fathers must seek ways to spend time with their children. The same is true for the millions of mothers who work out of the home and must face household chores upon their return, often at the expense of time devoted to their children or husbands.

Technology may change much of this, particularly for 30 to 40 percent of our work force. The booming computer field is now locating computer electronics in the home. Businessmen are beginning to find that many tasks can be accomplished just as well in the home as in the office. Salesmen, architects, writers, and many others are increasingly operating out of their homes, so why not computer programmers, operators, and some secretaries? With the high cost of energy expended to get to and from work, heating and air conditioning costs while there, plus the over one dollar per square foot of rent or cost for office space, we are rapidly coming to the place where on-line terminals, printing devices that can be activated from the home, and many future inventions will make it increasingly common for the home once again to become a center for both work and living.

Although all 8:00 A.M. to 5:00 P.M. labor will not be replaced, an increasing number of families in the future will find both husband and wife working in their own home, selling their output in the marketplace. This could eliminate the need for two cars, provide a parent to care for the children at all times, and serve to draw the family together.

As an employer I can foresee a tremendous advantage in the elimination of endless interruptions by other people. An incredible amount of productive time is lost in almost any business just by idle conversation. This is particularly true of Christian organizations, where "brotherly love" becomes a motivation for "fellowship" at company expense. I once watched a woman stop her work for twenty minutes to show another employee how to knit. Soon four other gals joined in for a lesson. Although they didn't realize it, that lesson cost their employer close to fifteen dollars. That is no great matter, until one multiplies such practices by 250 work days a year and the number of employees. A twenty-minute lunch in the kitchen or a snack while working is far more productive than a trip to the restaurant plus an hour or more for lunch. Fellowship is pleasant, but it creates an increasing problem for employers. Have you ever gone to the office or shop on Saturday or a holiday, when no one else was there, and found how much more work you could accomplish?

This idea of the electronic cottage won't catch on right away, but it is a wave of the future. An elaborate cottage schoolhouse may even become a reality in years to come. If the public schools continue to deteriorate in the next decade as they have in the past two, millions more parents will become disillusioned with our humanist-dominated and valueless public centers for education. With the prospects of backyard satellite TV about to burst onto the market, hundreds of TV channels will be available to every home. Some of these could be earmarked for education. Parents could pull educational institutions *of their choosing* into their homes, publishers could provide textbooks and workbooks, and children could learn at home, nullifying the need for millions of working mothers to leave the home to work. Perhaps small-group education could be set up in homes throughout the community. For example, Mrs. Smith down the street could pay a TV charge to bring in Channel 79, which contains instruction for the fourth graders, who come to her home daily. If tuition tax credits or some other form of reimbursement for private education could be legalized, the parents could pay Mrs. Smith for sending Johnny to her fourth-grade school—if they approved Mrs. Smith's educational qualifications, moral values, and standards of discipline. Parents have no such choices in today's humanist-dominated schools. The only alternative (if they are fortunate to live in the right area) is to send Johnny to a church or private school.

This cottage schoolhouse may be a futuristic idea, but it would certainly solve a number of problems: no busing; no sexually inflammatory courses; no antifamily teaching; closer control over the education of children by their parents; parental selection of their children's environment from 8:00 A.M. to 3:00 P.M.; a return to neighborliness as parents are drawn closer together; a job that does not require Mrs. Smith to leave home; smaller classes; and, best of all, the business of education (a $140-billion-a-year industry) placed on a competitive basis. Such competition in education would force the liberal humanists to stop using the public schools for the purpose of indoctrinating America's youth with their religious ideas (humanism is a religion [see *Battle for the Mind*]) and return to what they are being paid to do: help our children with the basics of reading, writing, and arithmetic. If children learn these basics, they can proceed to learn for themselves, if necessary, anything they need to know. If they don't assimilate these basics, their future learning will be seriously jeopardized. Lowering the standards for IQ tests, reading, and other basic skills, as modern "educators" are trying to do, will not change that fact.

At the risk of claiming to be a prophet, which I am not, I would like to predict that if the public schools are not purged of their unscientific notions of religious humanism and returned to a value-laden education, my eight-year-old granddaughter will send her children to a cottage schoolhouse or something better. America needs an educational system that is supportive of the family, not one that continually undermines the authority, values, and religious beliefs of the child's parents. To be so, it must be controlled by the family and designed to serve traditional family life.

Family Life in the 80s and 90s

Since it is impossible to eliminate the family without rendering mankind extinct, we might as well face it: The family is here to stay. Some will enjoy the kind of traditional family life Americans have always known. Others will be victims of the humanistic notions propounded in the many vehicles we have already examined. But each family will make its own choice, living by the precepts of humanism or building homes on principles of the Bible. Actually four basic kinds of families will be operative during the next few years.

1. The Humanist Family Life Liberal humanists, with many others, including hedonists, are committed to self-satisfaction. Obsessed with the idea that there is no God and that they are animals that evolved, these people postulate that "there are no absolutes." Consequently they can live any style of life that suits them. Self is the central concern of their philosophy. "If it feels good, do it!" "Do your own thing." "Satisfy yourself."

To such people marriage becomes optional, perversion is normal, and everything exists in a state of change. Consequently they do not start out assuming that marriage is permanent but, taking a cue from Toffler, anticipate four or five marriages in a given lifetime. Consequently there will continue to be an increase in trial marriages as a form of family. While such a family life-style may experience temporary moments of pleasure, it will also be filled with disappointment and heartache, for such anti-moral practices will lead to increased infidelity, perversion, alcoholism, violence, drug abuse, and even child abuse. Because of self-centeredness, childless families will increase.

How can we be so sure that humanistic policy will lead to such human chaos? Very simple. The Bible teaches that happiness does not just happen, but results from following the principles of God (Psalms 119:1, 2). It also promises, ". . . the way of transgressors is hard" (Proverbs 13:15). But as long as people are willing to sacrifice the permanent on the altar of the immediate, they will have to pay the price in "hard" living.

2. The Humanized Christian Family Life   We have already noted that there are degrees of humanism, just as there are degrees or variations among practicing Christians. The concepts of humanism are so prevalent in our society, from education to entertainment (even TV commercials reflect humanism's anti-moral philosophy), that many nonhumanists adopt some of its policies. Even unwary Christians, untaught or unwilling to submit to biblical principles, fall under its influence.

A humanized Christian is one who has professed faith in Christ but for some reason is so influenced by humanism that he acts more like a humanist than a Christian. Such a person often questions Christian principles and, in some cases, ridicules the church for its rigidity on principle. For example, he will question explicit, well-defined biblical precepts. "I don't see why I can't do my own thing and still be a good Christian." "Why do I have to attend church every week?" "I don't understand why I can't divorce my wife and marry someone else." One such individual, attempting to justify his lust, observed, "God loves me and wants me to be happy, but he knows my wife doesn't make me happy and my girl friend does, so I think it is God's will for me to divorce my wife and marry the woman I'm living with." The fact that God's Word expressly forbids such a decision is of little importance to him.

Essentially a humanized Christian does not bring himself under the authority of the Word of God but trusts the philosophy of humanism to produce happiness. The Bible warns such an individual, "There is a way which seemeth right unto a man, but the end thereof are the ways of death" (Proverbs 14:12). That person's life will be marred by chaos, and only God knows whether he is a humanist or a true Christian. At best he would be called a carnal Christian. Romans 8:6 (NAS) says, "For the mind set on the flesh is death. . . ." And his family life will reflect the degree of his carnality.

3. *Moralized Humanist Families* Not all humanists live like self-indulgent hedonists. Many will mirror or even adopt some of the moral values of the Judeo-Christian culture in which they were raised. I have met humanists who were faithful to their wives and had no thoughts of seeking another marriage. But idealistically they insisted on the right of every individual to choose for himself. Humanists *may* elect to be honest, dependable, moral, and upright; but that is optional for them. For Christians it is required.

The humanist politician is a good case in point. He often votes humanistically and lives morally, which is not inconsistent with the ideals of a humanist. His position also allows him to return to his congressional district and say, "I am personally in favor of the Right to Life Amendment, but I voted against it because I believe everyone should make his own decision." Whether that is campaign double-talk or his sincere belief, only he and God know.

The overwhelming majority of our population (84 percent of whom the Gallup Poll says still believe the Ten Commandments are valid) favor a moral view of the family. This certainly should include all born-again Christians, most Jews, and a large percentage of other religious adherents. Although they may not live up to the basic teachings of their faith all the time, it is their ordinary objective to do so. All such individuals enter marriage with a commitment to permanence, most of whom keep it; but even when they do not, they violate their own moral values. The success of their family life is dependent on how closely they adhere to their moral code.

4. *Spirit-Controlled Family Living* The ideal form of family life can never be governmentally established but is voluntarily assumed. Jesus Christ said, ". . . I am come that you might have life and that you might have it more *abundantly"* (*see* John 10:10). Next to the salvation experience itself, that abundant life is nowhere better illustrated over a lifetime than in a marriage relationship. For twenty-five years I pastored a large church in San Diego in which I saw many humanist families or humanized Christian families transformed into Spirit-controlled families. The transformation was from chaos to harmony. Oh, it didn't happen overnight, but it began with an acceptance of Christ personally and a commitment to let Him control their lives and home. This gradually produced the harmony, happiness, and fulfillment, which every human being desires for his family.

This ideal family life is outlined in Ephesians 5:18 through 6:4. Consider this synopsis:

> And do not be drunk with wine, in which is dissipation; but be filled with the Spirit, . . . submitting to one another in the fear of God. Wives, submit yourselves to your own husbands, as to the Lord. . . . Husbands, love your wives, just as Christ also loved the church and gave Himself for it. . . . Children, obey your parents in the Lord, for this is right. "Honor your father and mother," which is the first commandment with promise: "that it may be well with you and you may live long on the earth." And you fathers, do not provoke your children to wrath, but bring them up in the training and admonition of the Lord.
>
> Ephesians 5:18, 21, 22, 25; 6:1–4 NKJV–NT

When the Spirit of God controls a person and, through him, his family, that home, regardless of its circumstances, will experience the love, joy, and peace that everyone yearns for and that God promises (Galatians 5:22, 23). It is not automatic, but comes as the result of a day-by-day commitment to God and His principles.

Spirit-controlled family living follows six essential steps.

Step One: It begins with a genuine born-again experience with Jesus Christ on the part of both mother and father (John 3:3). Being born again is not a complex phenomenon. After all, our Lord said, ". . . unless you are converted and become as little children, you will by no means enter the kingdom of heaven" (Matthew 18:3 NKJV–NT). If it is easy enough for a child, it must not be very difficult. The key, however, is humility. Whenever a person humbles himself, acknowledges his sin to God, and repents of his selfish spirit, he can be *born again, converted,* or *saved.* These are synonymous terms.

One man in the New Testament sincerely repented by simply praying, ". . . God be merciful to me a sinner." Jesus said, ". . . this man went down to his house justified . . ." (Luke 18:13, 14). If you have never called on Jesus Christ or if you're not sure you have and would like to, I would suggest that if you pray a prayer similar to this, God promises to save you (Romans 10:9, 10:13; John 1:11):

> O God, I humbly admit I am a sinner and believe Jesus Christ died for me. I invite You into my life as Lord and Saviour and hereby give the control of my life to You. In Jesus' name I pray. Amen.

Once you have received Christ personally, you are then able to begin the Spirit-controlled life for yourself and your family.

Step Two: Make it your number-one priority to live to glorify God. Most people exist for their own satisfaction and glory. A Spirit-controlled Christian will seek to glorify his heavenly Father. As the Scripture teaches, "Therefore, whether you eat or drink, or whatever you do, do all to the glory of God" (1 Corinthians 10:31 NKJV–NT). No one can live the Spirit-controlled life who does not realize that man's primary purpose on earth is to glorify Him.

It is most difficult to get people to understand that self-indulgence will never bring satisfaction. Only an act of faith will create that awareness. A lifetime of glorifying God (pleasing Him in all that we do) brings the happiness and fulfillment people are seeking. (For further details see *Spirit-Controlled Family Living.*)

Step Three: A man and woman must be committed to each other for life. "You that are married, seek not to be loosed" (*see* 1 Corinthians 7:27).

God intended marriage to be a mental, emotional, and physical commitment for life. History shows that infidelity, adultery, polygamy, or even the system of having concubines, as followed by the Old Testament patriarchs, produced jealousy, friction, and heartache. As we face a future that is filled with accelerated moral temptation, couples need to realize that marriage is a commitment between God and each other "till death do us part."

Step Four: Families should have a desire for children. "Behold, children are a gift of the Lord; The fruit of the womb is a reward. Like arrows in the hand of a warrior, So are the children of one's youth" (Psalms 127:3, 4 NAS).

A noted authority (which usually means a humanist who has the ear of the media) was reported to have said, "By 1990 the population rate will drop to zero and most couples will remain childless." I often wonder if such comments are given newspaper coverage to report trends or help to create them. We have, however, seen a drastic decline in the birthrate, from 3.6 children per family in 1970, to 1.6 in 1980.

Children are not a biological accident, as some humanistically influenced people seem to imply. They are a blessing from the Lord. Choosing not to have children does not honor the will of God, but the will of humanism. Families are always enriched by children.

Step Five: The raising, training, disciplining, and discipling of children should be a major priority. "And you fathers, do not provoke your children to wrath, but bring them up in the training and admonition of the Lord" (Ephesians 6:4 NKJV–NT).

Anyone can propagate children; raising them takes responsibility. Therefore it is assumed that couples who get married should be old enough and mature enough to assume the responsibilities of parenthood, which is a natural result of marriage. Parenthood will require time spent with the children, not only for raising them and providing food, shelter, love, and attention, but for training them as we have previously outlined in this book. It will also involve discipline and discipling in the things of Jesus Christ. When parents spend the time to raise their children according to the precepts of their faith, then youngsters usually follow in their spiritual foot-steps. As the writer of Proverbs predicted, "Train up a child in the way he should go: and when he is old, he will not depart from it" (Proverbs 22:6).

Step Six: Spirit-controlled youth and children will obey their parents and the Lord. "Children, obey your parents in the Lord, for this is right. 'Honor your father and mother,' which is the first commandment with promise: 'that it may be well with you and you may live long on the earth' " (Ephesians 6:1–3 NKJV–NT).

Health and long life are promised both in the Old and New Testament to those children who honor and obey their parents. This is not for the pleasure of the parents, but in obedience to God and for the good of the child. The young person who learns to obey his parents early in life will not encounter trouble with the law when he leaves his home, nor will he find it difficult to submit in obedience to God.

The Secret to the Spirit-Controlled Life

Over sixteen years ago I wrote my first book on the Spirit-filled life. Since then I have had the privilege of sharing that subject with thousands of people. Through the years I have observed four keys to making the Spirit-controlled life an everyday reality for Christians.

1. A daily reading of the Bible (preferably the New Testament) and prayer.
2. A genuine commitment to doing whatever God instructs you to do through His Word and prayer.
3. Instant confession of any sin you commit, whether mental or physical.
4. A constant spirit of thanksgiving. "In everything give thanks; for this is the will of God in Christ Jesus for you" (1 Thessalonians 5:18 NKJV–NT).

What does family life in the 80s and 90s hold for you and your loved ones? That's up to you.

Note

1. Alvin Toffler, *Future Shock* (New York: Random House, 1970), pp. 203, 204.